T0036194

EDITED BY KAVEH AKBAR

The Penguin Book of Spiritual Verse

110 Poets on the Divine

PENGUIN BOOKS

PENGUIN CLASSICS

UK | USA | Canada | Ireland | Australia
India | New Zealand | South Africa

Penguin Books is part of the Penguin Random House group of companies
whose addresses can be found at global.penguinrandomhouse.com.

First published in Great Britain by Penguin Classics 2022
This edition published 2023
002

Editorial material and selection © Kaveh Akbar, 2022

The text on pp.343–356 constitutes an extension of this copyright page

The moral right of the editor has been asserted

Set in 10/13.75pt Warnock Pro
Typeset by Jouve (UK), Milton Keynes
Printed and bound in Great Britain by Clays Ltd, Elcograf S.p.A.

The authorized representative in the EEA is Penguin Random House Ireland,
Morrison Chambers, 32 Nassau Street, Dublin D02 YH68

A CIP catalogue record for this book is available from the British Library

ISBN: 978–0–241–39159–4

www.greenpenguin.co.uk

Penguin Random House is committed to a
sustainable future for our business, our readers
and our planet. This book is made from Forest
Stewardship Council® certified paper.

PENGUIN CLASSICS

THE PENGUIN BOOK OF SPIRITUAL VERSE

'If poetry is prayer, here are scriptures. Kaveh Akbar's brave,
encompassing map of spiritual hunger shows us that longing
belongs to all of us, whatever the languages we speak or
the geographies we inhabit' Jeet Thayil

'An amazing collection of spiritual verse from many cultures
and periods, from ancient Sumer in the third millennium
BCE up to the present. There cannot be any other
anthology that ranges so widely, and anyone concerned with
either poetry or spirituality will want to own a copy'
John Barton, author of *A History of the Bible:
The Book and Its Faiths*

'Wonderfully rich, this beautiful anthology of verse uniquely displays
how humans over centuries and across continents have wrestled
with the concept of the divine and, in turn, humanity's relation-
ship with that divinity. From exaltation to lament, from reflections
on beauty to explorations of science, these words draw the reader's
eyes towards the wonder of the numinous. A delightful celebration
of human creativity, with new insights from a trusted guide:
Kaveh Akbar' Chine McDonald, author of *God Is Not a
White Man: And Other Revelations*

'What an amazing compilation: beautifully edited, translated,
introduced, this book is far more than a typical poetry anthology.
What is it, then? It is our chance to overhear the splendid poet
Kaveh Akbar whisper to himself words which he lives by, as he
embarks on his own journey of spirit, loss, astonishment,
bewilderment, and, perhaps, understanding. The chorus of
voices gathered offer a balm, a consolation, a tune, in our
desolate world' Ilya Kaminsky, author of *Deaf Republic*

'How can language approach the spiritual – that which remains unlanguaged – and trace the limen between the self and what it falls silent before? In *The Penguin Book of Spiritual Verse*, Kaveh Akbar takes up this timeless inquiry with expansive curatorial shaping and heady joy, threading together Li Po and Adelia Prado, Hafez with Jabès, reverent with ludic, divine with corporeal, and everything that gets charged through, and between, them. These poems "thin the partition between a person and a divine," and they do so sublimely' Jenny Xie

'The choices Kaveh Akbar has made for this anthology of spiritual verse are spectacularly excellent. They are from regions of poetry at once accessible and exalted, representing the most intense of human experiences, the experiences of the divine, the yearning for the holy. Multiple cultures are represented: texts of ancient Mesopotamia, Egypt, Greece, Rome, the Arabic speaking world, the Farsi speaking world, poets of Hindi and Urdu, poets from everywhere in Asia, Africa, Europe, as well as England and the USA . . . There are several astonishing women, including Enheduanna, Mirabai, Gabriela Mistral. The book holds an embarrassment of riches, yet is light on its feet. You too will be smitten by the yearning that animates and drives these poems. Akbar's Introduction, and his notes on individual poems, are extra added value: the words of a poet' Alicia Ostriker, author of *The Volcano and After: Selected and New Poems, 2002–2019*

ABOUT THE AUTHOR

Kaveh Akbar is an Iranian American poet and scholar. He is the author of the poetry collections *Pilgrim Bell, Calling a Wolf a Wolf,* and *Portrait of the Alcoholic.* He teaches writing and Poetry of the Divine at Purdue University, Indiana.

for Paige

CONTENTS

INTRODUCTION

I was born in Tehran in 1989; my first two languages were Farsi and English. My third was Arabic, but Arabic gets an asterisk because I never really spoke it, I just learned to pray in it. Arabic was a private tongue reserved for God, God's own tongue, and I understood that if I spoke it to God earnestly, mellifluously, it would thin the membrane between us.

Today I have no idea what I mean when I say *God*, and I say it a lot.

The earliest attributable author in all of human literature is an ancient Sumerian priestess named Enheduanna. The daughter of King Sargon, Enheduanna wrote sensual, desperate hymns to the goddess Inanna: 'My beautiful mouth knows only confusion. / Even my sex is dust.' Written around 2300 BCE, Enheduanna's poems were the bedrock upon which much of ancient poetics was built. And her obsession? The precipitating subject of all our species' written word? Inanna, an ecstatic awe at the divine.

A year after I got sober, I learned from a routine physical that my liver was behaving abnormally, teetering on the precipice of pre-cirrhosis. This was after a year of excruciating recovery, a year in which nothing harder than Ibuprofen passed through my body. *If it's this bad after a year of healing*, a nurse told me, *imagine how bad it must have been a year ago when you quit.*

My earliest formulation of prayer was in Arabic, that beautiful, mysterious language of my childhood. I'd be called away from whatever trivia book I was reading or *Simpsons* episode I was watching to join my family in our ritual of collectively pushing these enigmatic sounds through our mouths. Moving through the postures of devotion in our kitchen, watching my older brother, my mother, my father, I had no idea what any of it meant, but I knew it all meant intensely.

When I got sober it wasn't because I punched a cop or drove my car into a Wendy's or anything dramatic like that. I had a dozen potential bottoms that would have awakened any reasonable person to the severity of the problem, but I was not a reasonable person. The day I finally lurched my way towards help was a day like any other. I woke up alone on my floor still drunk from the night before. I remember taking a pull or two from the nearly empty bottle of Old Crow bourbon by my mattress, then searching for my glasses and car keys. Finding them, I calmly drove myself to help.

Sappho was by all accounts one of history's greatest poets, but the entire corpus of her work burned with the great Library of Alexandria, so today we only know her through the bits other writers quoted. We know that in Fragment 22 she wrote:

> because I prayed
> this word:
> I want

but we don't have the entirety of the poem preceding it, her 'because' hanging there to explain some now unimaginable consequence of desire.

If my liver function was still so erratic after a year of healing, then at the end of my active addiction I must have been near some sort of Rubicon from which there could be no return. Some awareness permeated my dense fog of destruction. That awareness might have been bodily, the way an iron deficiency sometimes provokes in someone an unconscious desire to eat dirt. It might have been fatigue, a cumulative sense that the status quo of my living had become untenable. Or it might have been something else. I'll never know, which I think is the point.

From a poem of the Nahuatl people:

> This flesh, this clay of ours, is starved and trembling.
> And we, poor prisoners of our stomachs!
> There is nothing we can do.

A common formulation states that prayer is a way of speaking to the divine and meditation is a way of listening for it. Poetry synthesizes these, the silence of active composition being a time even the most sceptical writers describe using the language of the metaphysical, saying 'such-and-such a phrase *just came to me*', or 'those hours *just flew by*'. And then reading, a process through which dark runes on a page or strange vocalizations in the air can provoke us to laugh, weep, call our mothers, donate to Greenpeace or shiver with awe.

It is wrong to think of God as a debt to luck. But I could have died, and then I didn't. I haven't. When so many around me, like me, did and have.

One of the questions you can ask a poem is: to what do I owe my being here? Li Po: 'I sing, and moon rocks back and forth; / I dance, and shadow tumbles into pieces'. Gabriela Mistral: 'Sleeping, we made journeys / and arrived at no place'. Is it any wonder my former loadout of addictions, all narcotic, were sublimated into this new set of poetic obsessions and compulsions?

My working definition of sacred poetry rises directly out of my experience as a child praying in Arabic: earnest, musical language meant to thin the partition between a person and a divine, whether that divine is God or the universe or desire or land or family or justice or community or sex or joy or . . . As with my early prayers in Arabic, a one-to-one denotative understanding of the language isn't important – what matters is the making of music and the sincerity of the making.

When I was getting sober, I found no easy prayers, no poems to sing me well. What I did find was that, during the early days of my recovery, when sobriety was minute to minute – white knuckles and endless pacing and cheap coffee by the pot – poetry was a place I could put myself. I could read a book of poems and for an hour, two hours I didn't have to worry about accidentally killing myself. I could write a poem and the language for what was happening would *just come to me*. Hours would *just fly by*.

Rabi'a al-Basri, writing in the eighth century CE:

> Kings have locked their doors
> and each lover is alone with his love.
> Here, I am alone with You.

My active addiction was a time of absolute certainty – certainty of my own victimhood, of my convictions, of what I was owed by a universe that had split me from the land of my birth and dropped me into an America that was actively hostile to my presence. That certainty destroyed whatever it touched, corroding my own life and the lives of people who loved me. In recovery, when I threw myself into poetry, I was drawn to poems that were certain of nothing, poems that embraced mystery instead of trying to resolve it. Yeats:

> The ceremony of innocence is drowned;
> The best lack all conviction, while the worst
> Are full of passionate intensity.
> Surely some revelation is at hand.

Today the great weapon used to stifle critical thinking is a raw overwhelm of meaningless language at every turn – on our phones, on our TVs, in our periphery on billboards and subways. So often the language is passionately absolute: immigrants are evil, climate change is a hoax, and this new Rolex will make you sexually irresistible. Poetry opposes these things, asks us to slow down our metabolization of language, to become aware of it entering us. Sacred poetry teaches us to be comfortable with complexity, to be sceptical of unqualified certitude. In reminding us that language has history, density, integrity, such poetry is a potent antidote against a late-capitalist empire that would use empty, vapid language to cudgel us into inaction.

It is impossible to separate the part of me that is an addict-alcoholic from the part of me that experiences spiritual yearning, just as it's impossible to separate the part of me socialized as a Muslim American man. The same organ that wants me to drink controls my breathing and the contractions of my intestinal muscles. That same organ also reads the Quran and the Tao and the Psalms. It processes images of a rubbled Damascus, of a drone-struck wedding in Iraq. It also desires my spouse's touch, and marvels at the stars. There are no partitions between these realms of my consciousness, which is why my conception of sacred poetry includes not only explicitly metaphysical poets like Rabi'a and King David, but also poets like Anna Akhmatova, Marina Tsvetaeva, Edmond Jabès, Mahmoud Darwish and Lucille Clifton, poets for whom an exploration of the divine necessarily included explorations of the body and the body politic.

The great Persian poet Hafez wrote: 'Start seeing God everywhere, but keep it secret.' I still have no idea what I mean when I say God, but I see it everywhere. I mean it intensely. I write poems and, yes, books about it. I read about it constantly, which seems, counter-intuitively, only to deepen its secret.

I wanted to make this anthology because I wanted all these texts in one place. I claim no objectivity. These are 110 of my favourite attributed poems, texts that have been variously important and useful and illuminating for me across my living. Many will no doubt scan the table of contents and object to the omission of their favourite poet of the spirit, asking, 'Why Adélia Prado instead of Carlos Drummond de Andrade? Why Dickinson instead of Whitman?' Sometimes, the answer is boring: a finite permissions budget. But more often, such decisions are purely a function of which poets and poems have felt most essential to me, Kaveh Akbar, in my one vast and unprecedented life. I will say it again: I claim no objectivity.

Given this confession, though, I *will* say it was a goal to try to at least make a pass at accounting for the vast complexity of the human project of spiritual writing. Not to represent it, which, again, would take an Alexandrian Library or two. But to try to show confluences, overlaps of time and tone. In this anthology you'll find, for instance, that Dante Alighieri was born *while Rūmī was still alive and writing.* Or that 'American spiritual poetry' didn't begin with Dickinson or Whitman or anyone else writing in English, but with the Meso-American and Native people who inhabited the land that would be later called 'America', passing their sacred texts along for centuries. Relative to how long those texts were a part of the earth's spiritual history, Anglo-American texts are relatively brand new; the texts within this anthology are curated in rough proportion to that fact.

To flatten the project of 'spiritual poetry' to a bunch of white Romantic and Metaphysical poets is to erase the *Bhagavad Gita*, to wash away Li Po and Rabi'a and Mahadeviyakka and Teresa of Ávila and Bashō and Nâzim Hikmet. It's a colonization, one that erases not only the bodies and lands, but actual spirits. To the extent that there is any grand unified curatorial theory governing the content of this book, it exists in opposition to the colonial impulse.

Another load-bearing belief at work here: it's impossible to separate a spiritual poetics from the body that conceives it. Consider this moment from the *Popol Vuh*, the sixteenth-century Mayan creation narrative:

> It was simply the pure spirit
> and glinting spark of insight

of the Framer and the Shaper,
of Sovereign and Quetzal Serpent,

of She who has borne children,
and He who has planted them,

that framed and gave them shape.
They looked like true people,

and true people they became.
They spoke and they conversed.

They looked and they listened.
They walked and they grasped things,
and they held them in their hands.

They were excellent people,
well made and handsome.

They appeared with manly faces
and began to breathe,
and so they became

Often explorations of the divine move outwards with the language used to relay them – as our attention travels beyond our immediate bodily stations, so too do our voices, so too does our breath. The Arabic word *ruh* means both 'breath' and 'spirit', as does the Latin *spiritus*.

Collected here are 110 voices, each orbiting what G. K. Chesterton called the 'vertigo of the infinite', what Lucille Clifton called 'the lip of our understanding'. Not all of these poems are drawn from antiquity. Even today, when irony is the default posture of the public intellectual, many poets remain relentlessly sincere in their explorations of spiritual yearning (and spiritual doubt). Inquiries into the divine still connect contemporary poets to their ancestors. In one poem, the twelfth-century Kannada poet-saint Mahadeviyakka writes:

> When the body becomes Your mirror,
> how can it serve?
>
> When the mind becomes your mind,
> what is left to remember?

In her 'Astonishment', written over 800 years later, the twentieth-century Polish titan Wisława Szymborska seems almost to pick up where the ancient poet left off, wrapping question after question around the immobilizing strangeness of being anything:

> Why after all this one and not the rest?
> Why this specific self, not in a nest,
> but a house? Sewn up not in scales, but skin?
> Not topped off by a leaf, but by a face?

The mission of this anthology is to organize these connections – not to gather poets around geography or race or gender or belief or historical period, but instead around a shared privileging of the spirit and its attendant curiosities. In this way, readers might begin to hear a kind of conversation, one that has been ongoing for forty-three centuries and counting, a conversation into which countless young poets begin whispering every day.

Of course, no spirit lives in a vacuum. Some poets included in these pages, like Edmond Jabès, Anna Akhmatova and Nâzim Hikmet, fortified their spiritual poetics with blistering social critiques. Such poets, Carolyn Forché writes in *Poetry of Witness*, 'don't easily extricate morality, ethics, the sacred, and the political.

For them, it's not possible to think of these as isolated categories, but rather as modes of human contemplation and action which are inextricably bound to one another.' An attuned permeability to wonder compels the curious poet to rigorously examine their stations, both cosmic and civic.

For other poets like Sappho, Rūmī and Adélia Prado, divine and erotic loves braid together, creating a fully embodied devotion. Martin Buber wrote that God could be found only in other people – these poets would seem to agree. Consider Rūmī, who wrote:

> The stars will be watching us,
> and we will show them
> what it is to be a thin crescent moon.
> You and I unselfed.

Or Prado:

> The brush got old and no longer brushes.
> Right now what's important
> is to untangle the hair.
> We give birth to life between our legs
> and go on talking about it till the end,
> few of us understanding:
> it's the soul that's erotic.

The idea that ecstatic experience might (or must!) include the body is central to these poets; a quick glance at a dervish's whirling or a yogi's contorted meditation or shuckling during Jewish prayer will reveal several theological expressions of the same idea.

I have tried to account for these and countless other perspectives within the pages of this anthology. But comprehensively cataloguing forty-three centuries of spiritual writing is a fool's errand – there's too much to read in this or any lifetime, much less to accurately account for. Again, in just the thirteenth century alone, Mechthild of Magdeburg, Rūmī and Dante were living at the same time, gasping at the same stars – the mind reels!

Thus this anthology does not aim to represent holistically the entire corpus of human spiritual writing (the size of such a collection would be measured in libraries, not pages). Instead, it will attempt to call forth pivotal samples from my own reading and discovery that might present for readers a scale model of an ongoing human conversation. Other anthologies of sacred poetry have been mostly Eurocentric or male-dominated, in both poets and translators. This anthology aims to achieve a more universal perspective, privileging no single belief system or vantage point. In curating the anthology this way, I hope to advance for inspection a modest study in how poets across time and civilizations have wrapped language around our species' constant collective unknowable obsessions – doubt, the divine, and the wide, mysterious gulfs in between.

Kaveh Akbar, Indiana, 2022

Enheduanna
Twenty-third century BCE
From 'Hymn to Inanna'
Sumer
Translated by Jane Hirshfield

The Sumerian priestess Enheduanna is the earliest attributable author in all human literature. The daughter of King Sargon of Ur, she spent her life as a priestess to the goddess Inanna, writing hymns and epic verse. Despite being composed forty-three centuries ago, certain themes from her work has themes – ecological decimation, exile, God-hunger – that feel uncannily contemporary. Indeed, the centre of her poetic atom, the precipitating subject of all our species' writing, seems to be confusion, bewilderment, and a dizzy stagger at the divine.

Lady of all powers,
In whom light appears,
Radiant one
Beloved of Heaven and Earth,
Tiara-crowned
Priestess of the Highest God,
My Lady, you are the guardian
Of all greatness.
Your hand holds the seven powers:
You lift the powers of being,
You have hung them over your fingers,
You have gathered the many powers,
You have clasped them now
Like necklaces onto your breast.

Like a dragon,
You poisoned the land –
When you roared at the earth
In your thunder,
Nothing green could live.
A flood fell from the mountain:
You, Inanna,
Foremost in Heaven and Earth.
Lady riding a beast,
You rained fire on the heads of men.
Taking your power from the Highest,
Following the commands of the Highest,
Lady of all the great rites,
Who can understand all that is yours?

In the forefront
Of the battle,
All is struck down by you –
O winged Lady,
Like a bird
You scavenge the land.
Like a charging storm
You charge,
Like a roaring storm
You roar,
You thunder in thunder,
Snort in rampaging winds.
Your feet are continually restless.
Carrying your harp of sighs,
You breathe out the music of mourning.

It was in your service
That I first entered
The holy temple,
I, Enheduanna,
The highest priestess.
I carried the ritual basket,
I chanted your praise.
Now I have been cast out
To the place of lepers.
Day comes,
And the brightness
Is hidden around me.
Shadows cover the light,
Drape it in sandstorms.
My beautiful mouth knows only confusion.
Even my sex is dust.

Unknown
c. 2100 BCE
'Death of Enkidu', from *The Epic of Gilgamesh*
Babylon
Translated by N. K. Sanders

The Epic of Gilgamesh shapes all epics to come, including being a clear influence on The Iliad *and* The Odyssey. *In fact, certain scenes from* Gilgamesh *are almost directly mirrored: a magical woman who changes men into animals, dangerous trips to the Underworld. Though the hero Gilgamesh himself is presented in the text as 'two-thirds divine', the death of his beloved companion Enkidu shows that communion with a friend can be its own divine.*

This day on which Enkidu dreamed came to an end and he lay stricken with sickness. One whole day he lay on his bed and his suffering increased. He said to Gilgamesh, the friend on whose account he had left the wilderness, 'Once I ran for you, for the water of life, and I now have nothing.' A second day he lay on his bed and Gilgamesh watched over him but the sickness increased. A third day he lay on his bed, he called out to Gilgamesh, rousing him up. Now he was weak and his eyes were blind with weeping. Ten days he lay and his suffering increased, eleven and twelve days he lay on his bed of pain. Then he called to Gilgamesh, 'My friend, the great goddess cursed me and I must die in shame. I shall not die like a man fallen in battle; I feared to fall, but happy is the man who falls in the battle, for I must die in shame.' And Gilgamesh wept over Enkidu. With the first light of dawn he raised his voice and said to the counsellors of Uruk·

> 'Hear me, great ones of Uruk,
> I weep for Enkidu, my friend,
> Bitterly moaning like a woman mourning
> Weep for my brother.
> O Enkidu, my brother,
> You were the axe at my side,
> My hand's strength, the sword in my belt,
> The shield before me,
> A glorious robe, my fairest ornament;
> An evil Fate has robbed me.
> The wild ass and the gazelle
> That were father and mother,
> All long-tailed creatures that nourished you
> Weep for you,
> All the wild things of the plain and pastures;

The paths that you loved in the forest of cedars
Night and day murmur.
Let the great ones of strong-walled Uruk
Weep for you;
Let the finger of blessing
Be stretched out in mourning;
Enkidu, young brother. Hark,
There is an echo through all the country
Like a mother mourning.
Weep all the paths where we walked together;
And the beasts we hunted, the bear and hyena,
Tiger and panther, leopard and lion,
The stag and the ibex, the bull and the doe.
The river along whose banks we used to walk,
Weeps for you,
Ula of Elam and dear Euphrates
Where once we drew water for the water-skins.
The mountain we climbed where we slew the Watchman,
Weeps for you.
The warriors of strong-walled Uruk
Where the Bull of Heaven was killed,
Weep for you.
All the people of Eridu
Weep for you Enkidu.
Those who brought grain for your eating
Mourn for you now;
Who rubbed oil on your back
Mourn for you now;
Who poured beer for your drinking
Mourn for you now.
The harlot who anointed you with fragrant ointment
Laments for you now;
The women of the palace, who brought you a wife,

A chosen ring of good advice,
Lament for you now.
And the young men your brothers
As though they were women
Go long-haired in mourning.
What is this sleep which holds you now?
You are lost in the dark and cannot hear me.'

He touched his heart but it did not beat, nor did he lift his eyes again. When Gilgamesh touched his heart it did not beat. So Gilgamesh laid a veil, as one veils the bride, over his friend. He began to rage like a lion, like a lioness robbed of her whelps. This way and that he paced round the bed, he tore out his hair and strewed it around. He dragged off his splendid robes and flung them down as though they were abominations.

In the first light of dawn Gilgamesh cried out, 'I made you rest on a royal bed, you reclined on a couch at my left hand, the princes of the earth kissed your feet. I will cause all the people of Uruk to weep over you and raise the dirge of the dead. The joyful people will stoop with sorrow; and when you have gone to the earth I will let my hair grow long for your sake, I will wander through the wilderness in the skin of a lion.' The next day also, in the first light, Gilgamesh lamented; seven days and seven nights he wept for Enkidu, until the worm fastened on him. Only then he gave him up to the earth, for the Anunnaki, the Judges, had seized him.

Unknown
Sixteenth century BCE
From *The Book of the Dead*
Egypt
Translated by Alexandre Piankoff

The ancient Egyptian Book of the Dead *was a compendium
of charms and spells designed to help the recently deceased
move through the next world. One passage from our included
excerpt begins, 'These gods are like this.' How much of humanity's
wondering, grief, war can be tracked to their certitudes in
responding to that single utterance?*

Egyptian God Names

1.

'It is Re who created his names out of his members'

2.

These gods are like this in their caverns, which are in the Netherworld. Their bodies are in darkness.

The Upreared One.
Cat.
Terrible One.
Fat Face.
Turned Face.
The One belonging to the Cobra.

3.

They are like this in their coffins. They are the rays of the Disk, their souls go in the following of the Great God.

The One of the Netherworld.
The Mysterious One.
The One of the Cavern.
The One of the Coffin.
She who combs.
The One of the Water.
The Weaver.

4.

These gods are like this: they receive the rays of the Disk when it lights up the bodies of those of the Netherworld. When he passes by, they enter into darkness.

The Adorer.
Receiving Arm.
Arm of Light.
Brilliant One.
The One of the Rays.
Arm of Dawn.

5.

Salutations to Osiris.

Osiris the Gold of Millions.
Osiris the Great Saw.
Osiris the Begetter.
Osiris the Scepter.
Osiris the King.
Osiris on the Sand.
Osiris in all the Lands.
Osiris at the head of the Booth of the distant Marshlands.
Osiris in his places which are in the South.
Osiris at the head of his town.

6.

The Cat.

Head of Horus.
Face of Horus.
Neck of Horus.
Throat of Horus.
Iii.
The Gory One.

7.

The Swallower of Millions.

Unknown
Tenth century BCE
Song of Songs, chapters 1 and 2
Kingdom of Israel
From the King James Version of the Bible

*Song of Songs (also called Song of Solomon) is a strange interlude
in the Hebrew Bible, less about the laws of man or God's terrible
power and more about celebrating corporeal, deeply embodied
love, sexual and romantic love between lovers so intense it
becomes divine. The language of Song of Songs can still be heard
in our contemporary romantic idiom – 'I have compared thee, O
my love, to a company of horses in Pharaoh's chariots' finds an
echo in Shakespeare's 'Shall I compare thee to a summer's day?'.*

The song of songs, which is Solomon's.

Let him kiss me with the kisses of his mouth: for thy love is better than wine.

Because of the savour of thy good ointments thy name is as ointment poured forth, therefore do the virgins love thee.

Draw me, we will run after thee: the king hath brought me into his chambers: we will be glad and rejoice in thee, we will remember thy love more than wine: the upright love thee.

I am black, but comely, O ye daughters of Jerusalem, as the tents of Kedar, as the curtains of Solomon.

Look not upon me, because I am black, because the sun hath looked upon me: my mother's children were angry with me; they made me the keeper of the vineyards; but mine own vineyard have I not kept.

Tell me, O thou whom my soul loveth, where thou feedest, where thou makest thy flock to rest at noon: for why should I be as one that turneth aside by the flocks of thy companions?

If thou know not, O thou fairest among women, go thy way forth by the footsteps of the flock, and feed thy kids beside the shepherds' tents.

I have compared thee, O my love, to a company of horses in Pharaoh's chariots.

Thy cheeks are comely with rows of jewels, thy neck with chains of gold.

We will make thee borders of gold with studs of silver.

While the king sitteth at his table, my spikenard sendeth forth the smell thereof.

A bundle of myrrh is my wellbeloved unto me; he shall lie all night betwixt my breasts.

My beloved is unto me as a cluster of camphire in the vineyards of En-gedi.

Behold, thou art fair, my love; behold, thou art fair; thou hast doves' eyes.

Behold, thou art fair, my beloved, yea, pleasant: also our bed is green.

The beams of our house are cedar, and our rafters of fir.

I am the rose of Sharon, and the lily of the valleys.

As the lily among thorns, so is my love among the daughters.

As the apple tree among the trees of the wood, so is my beloved among the sons. I sat down under his shadow with great delight, and his fruit was sweet to my taste.

He brought me to the banqueting house, and his banner over me was love.

Stay me with flagons, comfort me with apples: for I am sick of love.

His left hand is under my head, and his right hand doth embrace me.

I charge you, O ye daughters of Jerusalem, by the roes, and by the hinds of the field, that ye stir not up, nor awake my love, till he please.

The voice of my beloved! behold, he cometh leaping upon the mountains, skipping upon the hills.

My beloved is like a roe or a young hart: behold, he standeth behind our wall, he looketh forth at the windows, shewing himself through the lattice.

My beloved spake, and said unto me, Rise up, my love, my fair one, and come away.

For, lo, the winter is past, the rain is over and gone;

The flowers appear on the earth; the time of the singing of birds is come, and the voice of the turtle is heard in our land;

The fig tree putteth forth her green figs, and the vines with the tender grape give a good smell. Arise, my love, my fair one, and come away.

O my dove, that art in the clefts of the rock, in the secret places of the stairs, let me see thy countenance, let me hear thy voice; for sweet is thy voice, and thy countenance is comely.

Take us the foxes, the little foxes, that spoil the vines: for our vines have tender grapes.

My beloved is mine, and I am his: he feedeth among the lilies. Until the day break, and the shadows flee away, turn, my beloved, and be thou like a roe or a young hart upon the mountains of Bether.

King David
c. 1000 BCE
Psalm 23
Kingdom of Israel
From the King James Version of the Bible

David wore a million hats – warrior, theologian, king – but he was also, critically, a poet. His ability to write simple and unmistakable music into his Psalms – music that survives centuries and translations – preserves them. David's strength wasn't just his might or mind, but also his ear. The music of the Psalms gave them their radical endurance.

The Lord is my shepherd; I shall not want.

He maketh me to lie down in green pastures: he leadeth me beside the still waters.

He restoreth my soul: he leadeth me in the paths of righteousness for his name's sake.

Yea, though I walk through the valley of the shadow of death, I will fear no evil: for thou art with me; thy rod and thy staff they comfort me.

Thou preparest a table before me in the presence of mine enemies: thou anointest my head with oil; my cup runneth over.

Surely goodness and mercy shall follow me all the days of my life: and I will dwell in the house of the Lord for ever.

Homer
Ninth or eighth century BCE
From *The Odyssey*
Greece
Translated by Emily Wilson

A funny thing, to begin an epic like The Odyssey *with the gods complaining about the humans' complaining. Emily Wilson talks about how she imagines Homer as a 'they', possibly a committee of ungendered persons arriving upon a text together. Mortals who blame the gods for their suffering, but then 'increase it by folly'.*

                            'This is absurd,
that mortals blame the gods! They say we cause
their suffering, but they themselves increase it
by folly. So Aegisthus overstepped:
he took the legal wife of Agamemnon,
then killed the husband when he came back home,
although he knew that it would doom them all.
We gods had warned Aegisthus; we sent down
perceptive Hermes, who flashed into sight
and told him not to murder Agamemnon
or court his wife; Orestes would grow up
and come back to his home to take revenge.
Aegisthus would not hear that good advice.
But now his death has paid all debts.'

                                  Athena
looked at him steadily and answered, 'Father,
he did deserve to die. Bring death to all
who act like him! But I am agonizing
about Odysseus and his bad luck.
For too long he has suffered, with no friends,
sea all around him, sea on every side,
out on an island where a goddess lives,
daughter of fearful Atlas, who holds up
the pillars of the sea, and knows its depths –
those pillars keep the heaven and earth apart.
His daughter holds that poor unhappy man,
and tries beguiling him with gentle words
to cease all thoughts of Ithaca; but he
longs to see even just the smoke that rises
from his own homeland, and he wants to die.

You do not even care, Olympian!
Remember how he sacrificed to you
on the broad plain of Troy beside his ships?
So why do you dismiss Odysseus?'

'Daughter!' the Cloud God said, 'You must be joking,
since how could I forget Odysseus?
He is more sensible than other humans,
and makes more sacrifices to the gods.
But Lord Poseidon rages, unrelenting,
because Odysseus destroyed the eye
of godlike Polyphemus, his own son,
the strongest of the Cyclopes – whose mother,
Thoösa, is a sea-nymph, child of Phorcys,
the sea king; and she lay beside Poseidon
inside a hollow cave. The Lord of Earthquakes
prevents Odysseus from reaching home
but does not kill him. Come then, we must plan:
how can he get back home? Poseidon must
give up his anger, since he cannot fight
alone against the will of all the gods.'

Sappho
c. 630–570 BCE
Fragments 22 and 118
Greece
Translated by Anne Carson

*The entire corpus of Sappho's work burned with the great
Library of Alexandria, so today we know her only through the
bits other writers quoted, shadows of Sappho cast on our cave
wall. Time marbled silence throughout the texts, and those gaps,
those cavities, beg readers to wonder them full, to complete the
poet's circuits of cognition – twenty-six centuries after they were
made.*

22

```
                    ]
                    ] work
                    ] face
                    ]
                    ]
                    if not, winter
                    ] no pain
                    ]
]I bid you sing
of Gongyla, Abanthis, taking up
your lyre as (now again) longing
          floats around you,
```

you beauty. For her dress when you saw it
stirred you. And I rejoice.
In fact she herself once blamed me
          Kyprogeneia

because I prayed
this word:
I want

118

yes! radiant lyre speak to me
become a voice

Patacara
Sixth century BCE
India
Translated by Susan Murcott

*'I'm not lazy or proud.' writes Patacara, an ancient disciple of
the Buddha, 'Why haven't I found peace?' Her simple clarity
astonishes, as does the final movement here. What do darkness,
stillness, silence make possible?*

When they plow their fields
and sow seeds in the earth,
when they care for their wives and children,
young brahmans find riches.

But I've done everything right
and followed the rule of my teacher.
I'm not lazy or proud.
Why haven't I found peace?

Bathing my feet
I watched the bathwater
spill down the slope.
I concentrated my mind
the way you train a good horse.

Then I took a lamp
and went into my cell,
checked the bed,
and sat down on it.
I took a needle
and pushed the wick down.

When the lamp went out
my mind was freed.

Lao Tzu
Fifth century BCE
'Easy by Nature', from *Tao Te Ching*
China
Translated by Ursula K. Le Guin

*Le Guin's translation of Lao Tzu preserves the original's
crystalline clarity – we meet the language in motion, flowing,
elemental, like laughter passing between friends, or water moving
over land. Another section of the* Tao *describes the seven noble
virtues of water, including its unconditional administration –
water doesn't discriminate between anyone or anything. It gives
itself freely to all it encounters.*

Easy by Nature

True goodness
is like water.
Water's good
for everything.
It doesn't compete.

It goes right
to the low loathsome places,
and so finds the way.

For a house,
the good thing is level ground.
In thinking,
depth is good.
The good of giving is magnanimity;
of speaking, honesty;
of government, order.
The good of work is skill,
and of action, timing.

No competition,
so no blame.

Chandaka
Sixth century BCE
Two Cosmologies
India
Translated by W. S. Merwin and J. Moussaieff Masson

Chandaka, like Patacara, was a personal disciple of the Buddha.
He worked as a royal charioteer, a kind of ancient limo driver.
But in his own time he penned eternal verse such as we've
excerpted here, exploring the more human qualities of his divines.
Mischievous Krishna, he eats dirt and makes the universe inside
his mouth!

Two Cosmologies

1

The goddess Laksmi
Loves to make love to Vishnu
from on top
looking down she sees in his navel
a lotus
and on it Brahma the god
but she can't bear to stop
so she puts her hand
over Vishnu's right eye
which is the sun
and night comes on
and the lotus closes
with Brahma inside

2

Krishna went out to play
Mother
and he ate dirt

Is that true Krishna

No
who said it

Your brother Balarama

Not true
Look at my face

Open your mouth.

      he opened it
and she stood speechless

inside was
the universe

may he protect you

Vyasa
c. 400 BCE
From the *Bhagavad Gita*
India
Translated by Laurie L. Patton

Like many ancient spiritual texts, the Bhagavad Gita, *itself part of the larger Hindi epic* Mahabarata, *functions both as an epic narrative and a guide for practical living.* Gita *means 'song'; the text can be sung as means of remembering, or meditating upon, its lessons. Our brief excerpt, from Chapter 3, manages to capture several of the major themes of the text: oneness, eternity, wisdom, non-attachment.*

16

The one who does not
set the wheel
in motion
here on earth
lives uselessly,
wanting to hurt,
impassioned by the senses,
Son of Pritha.

17

The person
who would be content
in the self,
pleased in the self,
happy in the self –
for that one,
a reason for action
does not exist.

18

For that person,
there is no goal in action,
nor any goal
in non-action;
and that one

does not cling to goals,
in connection with
any beings.

19

So, without clinging,
always perform
actions to be done.
When one performs
actions to be done
without clinging,
one attains
the highest.

20

By action alone,
King Janaka
and many others
gained fulfilment.
observing even
the simple maintenance
of the world,
you should act!

21

As the best person
practices

in various pursuits,
so too will the rest.
That one sets
the standard
that the world
then follows.

22

Son of Pritha:
for me, nothing at all
is to be done
in the three worlds;
there is nothing
to be reached
which has not been reached.
Even so, I move in action.

23

Surely if I,
who am inexhaustible,
did not undertake
any action at all,
humankind would
follow my path
everywhere,
Son of Pritha.

24

If I did not
perform actions,
these worlds
would sink down;
I would be a creator
of scattered confusion,
and I would destroy
these human beings.

25

Son of Bharata,
just as the unwise ones act
while clinging to action,
so the wise should act
without clinging,
but rather, wanting
to keep the world
collected together.

Lucretius
First century BCE
From *The Nature of Things*
Ancient Rome
Translated by A. E. Stallings

The poet and philosopher Lucretius writes prophetically here about an endlessly expanding universe. Two short millennia later, modern astronomers would arrive at a similar model.

But since I've taught that atoms are as solid as can be,
And flit, unconquered, endlessly throughout eternity,
Come now, let us unfurl if there is any upper bound
To their sum, and also as regards that void that we have found
Exists – place or space where each thing comes to pass – let's see
Whether its extent is bounded fundamentally,
Or else it opens measureless and fathomlessly deep.
The universe must therefore have no limits in its sweep
In all directions, for if it did, then it would have a bound,
And if it has a boundary, then something must surround
It from without, so that the eye can follow only so
Far and no farther. And since we must confess that there is no
Thing *beyond* the universe, then it can have no border,
And stretches limitless and without end. Whatever quarter
You stand in makes no difference. Whatever place you are,
It stretches out in all directions infinitely far.
But let's say for a moment Space *were* limited. Pretend
That someone with a spear goes running to the very end
And hurls the whizzing missile. Does the spinning spear then go
Flying afar along the trajectory of the mighty throw,
Or do you think that something thwarts it, standing in its path?
You must confess just one of these is true – you can't have both –
Yet each shuts your escape hatch and compels you to confess,
Whichever one you choose, the universe is limitless.
For whether there is something there to thwart the missile's flight
So it falls short of its target, or it passes on outside,
It was not launched from any boundary. I'll persevere:
Wherever you set the furthest brink, I'll ask about the spear.
The result is that no last frontier can ever stay in place –
For possible flight forever pushes back the edge of Space.

Furthermore, if all of Space were limited and bound
With definite boundaries on every side the whole way round,
By this time, sinking underneath its solid weight, the store
Of matter would have sifted from every side down to the floor
Of the universe. Nor could anything at all be done
Under the tent of heaven; there would be no shining sun,
Nor any heaven either. Instead, there would only lie a vast
Heap of matter, sunken down through endless ages past.
But as things stand, the basic particles are not allowed
Any respite, since the universe is not endowed
With any fundament at all, no place where they might flow
Down to and settle. But always, every thing is on the go
In every corner, and atoms are supplied and ever flit,
Stirred up ceaselessly, out of the bottomless Infinite.

Virgil
70–19 BCE
From *The Aeneid*
Ancient Rome
Translated by Sarah Ruden

In this early passage of The Aeneid *we see the gods in conversation about the most human of emotions – envy, fear, entitlement, parental concern. To assuage his daughter's anxieties, Jove begins to tell the story of what will set up the rest of Virgil's epic poem.*

The day was over. Jove looked down from heaven
At the sail-flying waters, outstretched lands
And shores, and far-flung nations. At the sky's peak,
He fixed his gaze on Libyan territory.
His mind was anxious, busy. And now Venus
Spoke these sad words to him, her shining eyes
Filling with tears, 'You, everlasting ruler
Of gods and men and fearful lightning-thrower,
What great crime did Aeneas and the Trojans
Commit against you? They have died and died,
But in the whole world found no Italy.
You promised that the circling years would draw
Teucer's new lineage from them, Romans, chieftains,
To rule an empire on the land and sea.
Father, what new thought turns you from this purpose?
When Troy calamitously fell, I weighed it
Against the fate to come, to my great comfort.
And yet the pummeling fortunes of these heroes
Don't change. When will you end their trials, great ruler?
Antenor could escape the swarm of Greeks;
Into Illyrian coves, into Liburnia.
He safely voyaged, to the Timavus' source.
Where the sea breaks through nine mouths, and the mountain
Roars, and the echoing waves oppress the fields.
And here he founded Padua, a homeland
For Trojans, with a Trojan name, its gateway
Displaying Trojan arms. He has his rest there.
But we, your children, promised heirs to heaven,
Have lost our ships – obscene! – through Someone's anger
And treachery. We are kept from Italy.
Is this our new realm, won through righteousness?'

The gods' and mortals' father gave his daughter
The smile that clears the sky of storms and kissed her
Lightly, and this was how he answered her:
'Take heart – no one will touch the destiny
Of your people. You will see Lavinium
In its promised walls, and raise your brave Aeneas
To the stars. No new thoughts change my purposes.
But since you suffer, I will tell the future,
Opening to the light fate's secret book.
In Italy your son will crush a fierce race
In a great war.

Shenoute
c. 360–*c.* 450 CE
'Homily'
Egypt

A great Coptic saint, Shenoute is also one of the titans of Coptic literature. Here is a simple and short sermon against idolaters and heretics.

Homily

Regarding the sinners,
the pagans and heretics:
they ignore all we say.
The shameless evil-hearted,
filthy with ignorance of the One.
Run away, men of God,
run from their trap,
from the heathens, run
from evil!

Sengcan
c. 496–606
'The Mind of Absolute Trust'
China
Translated by Stephen Mitchell

A religious descendant of the Buddha, Sengcan writes: 'One is all; all are one. When you realize this, what reason for holiness or wisdom?' Here, as in many other ancient spiritual texts, we see wisdom and holiness set against each other; no clear winner emerges.

The Mind of Absolute Trust

The Great Way isn't difficult
    for those who are unattached to their preferences.
Let go of longing and aversion,
    and everything will be perfectly clear.
When you cling to a hairbreadth of distinction,
    heaven and earth are set apart.
If you want to realize the truth,
    don't be for or against.
The struggle between good and evil
    is the primal disease of the mind.
Not grasping the deeper meaning,
    you just trouble your mind's serenity.
As vast as infinite space,
    it is perfect and lacks nothing.
But because you select and reject,
    you can't perceive its true nature.
Don't get entangled in the world;
    don't lose yourself in emptiness.
Be at peace in the oneness of things,
    and all errors will disappear by themselves.

If you don't live the Tao,
    you fall into assertion or denial.
Asserting that the world is real,
    you are blind to its deeper reality;
denying that the world is real,
    you are blind to the selflessness of all things.
The more you think about these matters,
    the farther you are from the truth.
Step aside from all thinking,
    and there is nowhere you can't go.

Returning to the root, you find the meaning;
     chasing appearances, you lose their source.
At the moment of profound insight,
     you transcend both appearance and emptiness.
Don't keep searching for the truth;
     just let go of your opinions.

For the mind in harmony with the Tao,
     all selfishness disappears.
With not even a trace of self-doubt,
     you can trust the universe completely.
All at once you are free,
     with nothing left to hold on to.
All is empty, brilliant,
     perfect in its own being.
In the world of things as they are,
     there is no self, no non-self.
If you want to describe its essence,
     the best you can say is "Not-two."
In this "Not-two" nothing is separate,
     and nothing in the world is excluded.
The enlightened of all times and places
     have entered into this truth.
In it there is no gain or loss;
     one instant is ten thousand years.
There is no here, no there;
     infinity is right before your eyes.
The tiny is as large as the vast
     when objective boundaries have vanished;
the vast is as small as the tiny
     when you don't have external limits.
Being is an aspect of non-being;
     non-being is no different from being.

Until you understand this truth,
    you won't see anything clearly.
One is all; all
    are one. When you realize this,
    what reason for holiness or wisdom?
The mind of absolute trust
    is beyond all thought, all striving,
is perfectly at peace, for in it
    there is no yesterday, no today, no tomorrow.

From the Quran
610–632
Mecca
Translated by Muhammad Muhsin Khan and Muhammad
Taqi-ud-Din al-Hilali

*In Islam, the Quran is believed to be the direct word of God as
transmitted to the Prophet Muhammad by the Angel Gabriel.
Attributing this excerpt correctly, then, demands we attribute
it to the Abrahamic God Himself, not the Prophet. Also worth
noting: the Quran expressly states that it is not poetry – 'As for
poets, only the misguided follow them' – but I felt a curatorial
affordance for this bit of non-poetry was justified.*

Did We not expand for you, [O Muhammad], your breast?
And We removed from you your burden
Which had weighed upon your back
And raised high for you your repute.
For verily, with hardship comes ease.
Verily, with hardship comes ease.
So when you have finished [your duties], then stand up [for worship]
And direct your longing to your Lord.

Kakinomoto Hitomaro
c. 653–c. 708
'In praise of Empress Jitō'
Japan
Translated by Geoffrey Bownas and Anthony Thwaite

Hitomaro was Empress Jitō's court poet. In this piece we see a complete conflation of political and cosmic power – 'True god of true god'. Jitō's political station becomes its own divine.

In praise of Empress Jitō

Our great Empress
Who rules in tranquillity,
True god of true god,
Has done a divine thing.
Deep in the valley
Of Yoshino's foaming torrents
She builds high
Her tall palace.

She climbs and looks
Across her lands:
The mountain folds,
Like green walls,
As offerings
From their deity,
When spring comes
Bring cherry garlands:
When autumn begins
They bring crimson leaves.
The river spirit too
Makes gifts of sacred food:
In the upper shoals
He sets the cormorants,
In the lower shallows
He spreads small nets.
Mountain and river too
Come near and serve
This godlike land.

Li Po
701–762
'Drinking Alone Beneath the Moon'
China
Translated by David Hinton

*According to legend, Li Po died when one night, drunk and alone
in his canoe, he saw the moon's reflection on the water, dived in
after it and drowned.*

Drinking Alone Beneath the Moon

Among the blossoms, a single jar of wine.
No one else here, I ladle it out myself.
Raising my cup, I toast the bright moon,
and facing my shadow makes friends three,
though moon has never understood wine,
and shadow only trails along behind me.
Kindred a moment with moon and shadow,
I've found a joy that must infuse spring:
I sing, and moon rocks back and forth;
I dance, and shadow tumbles into pieces.
Sober, we're together and happy. Drunk,
we scatter away into our own directions:
intimates forever, we'll wander carefree
and meet again in Star River distances.

Rabi'a al-Basri
c. 717–801
Iraq
Translated by Charles Upton

*Freed from slavery at a young age, when her master saw her
praying alone surrounded by celestial light, Rabi'a became an
early Muslim ascetic, spiritual leader and poet. Late in her life,
when asked about the origin of her wisdom, she replied: 'You
know of the how, I know of the how-less.'*

O my Lord,
the stars glitter
and the eyes of men are closed.
Kings have locked their doors
and each lover is alone with his love.

Here, I am alone with You.

Ono No Komachi
c. 825–c. 900
Japan
Translated by Jane Hirshfield

Ancient Japanese waka *poets often worked in a 5-7-5-7-7 metre. This gorgeous poem by the* waka *poet Ono No Komachi reminds me of an old Persian parable I heard in my youth. A holy man had renounced all his worldly possessions, knowing he needed nothing to pray and live with save his old, chipped water bowl. One day at the river he saw a young boy drinking water from his cupped hands. The holy man was so humbled that, admonished, he immediately gave away his water bowl and returned home.*

This inn
on the road to Iwanoue
is a cold place to sleep . . .
Oh monk,
would you please lend me your robes?

The monk's reply:

Those who have given up the world
wear only a single layer
of moss-rough cloth,
yet not to offer it would be heartless.
Let us sleep together, then.

Hanshan
Ninth century
'Hanshan's Poem'
China
Translated by A. S. Kline

Hanshan was a hermit-poet who often wrote drafts on stones and scraps of leaves. Like the beauty of the peach petals in this poem, most of his work has been lost to the ages.

The peach petals would like to stay,
But moon and wind blow them on.
You won't find those ancient men,
Those dynasties are dead and gone.
Day by day the blossoms fall,
Year by year the people go.
Where the dust blows through these heights,
There once shone a silent sea.

Al-Husayn ibn Ahmad ibn Khalawayh
Tenth century
'Names of the Lion'
Syria
Translated by David Larsen

In this poem, al-Husayn ibn Ahmad ibn Khalawayh plays with the Islamic trope of ninety-nine names of God presented in the Quran, here applying the same treatment to 'the most fearsome' lion, great divine of the wild.

Names of the Lion

al-Waththāb	'The Pouncer'
al-ʿAḍūḍ	'The Distresser'
al-Mihzaʿ	'The Smasher'
al-Miktal	'The Big Food-Basket'
al-ʿAkammash	'Whose Numbers Are Oppressive'
al-Muḥrib	'The Belligerent'
al-Sāriḥiyy	'The Pastoral [Scourge]'
al-Muḍāmiḍ	'The Open-Mouthed'
al-Qaʿfāniyy	'Whose Tread Stirs the Dust' (?)
al-Hijaff	'The Imposing Bulk'
al-ʿAssās	'Who Looks for Trouble in the Night'
al-Mukhayyas	'Whose Den Is Well Kept'
al-Sawwār	'Who Goes Straight for the Head'
al-Musāfir	'The Wayfarer'
al-Ṭaḥḥār	'Whose Eyes Burn'
al-Ghayyāl	'The Well-Concealed'
al-Miṣakk	'The Slammer'
al-Ahyab	'The Most Fearsome'
Dhū Libd	'Whose Hair is Matted'
al-Dilhām	'The Dusky'
al-Hawātima	'Terror of the Lowland' (?)
al-Arash	'The Raking Blow'
al-Shaddākh	'The Skull Crusher'
al-Dilhātha	'Who Strides Unflinching into Battle'
al-Qanawṭar	'The Impaler' (?), said also of the male member of the tortoise, and the spear
Dhu 'l-ʿUfra	'Whose Hair Gets Thicker When He's Mad'
Dhu 'l-Khīs	'Who Has a Hiding Place'
Layth al-ʿArīn	'Lion of the Treetop Hideaway'
Layth Khaffān	'Lion of the Lion-Infested Area'
Layth al-Ghāb	'Lion of the Thicket'

Nazij	'Prancer'
Akhram	'Hare-Lip'
al-Shābil	'Whose Teeth Are Interlaced'
al-A'far	'Whose Coat Is the Color of the Surface of the Earth'
al-Midlāj	'Who Shows up Late at Night'
al-Mawthabān	'The Seated [Monarch]', also a title of the Ḥimyarites for a king who never stirs from atop his throne
al-Dawsar	'The Lusty'
al-Abghath	'Whose Coat Is Ashy'
al-Aghthā	'Whose Coat Is Shabby'
al-Ghathawthar	'The Thug'
al-Ghuthāghith	'Who Fights without a Weapon'
al-Ghāzī	'The Morning Apparition'
al-Mufarfir	'The Mangler'
al-Khashshāf	'The Calamity'
al-Azhar	'The Radiant'
al-Irrīs	'The Chief'
al-Ajwaf	'The Big-Bellied'
al-Jāfī	'The Brute'
al-Jāhil	'The Unrepentant'
al-Mu'lankis	'Whose Hair Hangs in Clusters'
al-Jayfar	'Whose Sides Are Well Filled Out'
al-Māḍī	'The Cutter', also said of a sword
al-Quṣquṣa	'The Stocky'
al-Ḍārī	'The Blood-Bather', also said of an open vein
al-Ṣabūr	'The Perseverant'
al-Ṣa'b	'The Difficult'
al-Muḥtajir	'Furiously Jealous in Defense of What Is His'
al-Mudill	'The Brazen'
al-Hayṣama	'The Destroyer'
al-Ashra'	'Whose Nose Is Long and Prominent'

al-Qaḍūḍ	'The Sunderer'
al-Ḍubāḍib	'The Giant Lout'
al-Qirḍim	'Who Takes the Whole'
al-Ruzam	'Who Can't Be Budged'
al-Hajjās	'The Show-Off'
al-Muqaṣmil	'The Brutal Shepherd'
al-'Antarīs	'Valiant in Battle,' [said for] the lion and the she-camel
al-Shaykh	'The Elder'

Unknown
975
Anglo-Saxon charm
Translated by Jos Charles

*For some cultures, a poem could be a divine chant activated by
its own sound, simply by virtue of being in the air. It could also
hold valuable medicinal information, like this one on how to treat
cancerous growths.*

Against A Growth

Cancer, cancer,   excrete of cancer,
not in timber stock   nor field of bone
but north you head   to a heap
where, little spume,   a brother exists.
There put   sprig on its head.
Under wolves' feet, under the eagle barb,
under one eagle claw   you waste,
clung up as char   on the hearth,
shrunk dry, some dung   on the wall,
eroding   like water in its basin.
So, little you, exist   like linseed corn,
waste to the hipbone of a hand maggot,
until, little you, exist   as nothing exists.

Izumi Shikibu
c. 976–*c.* 1030
'Things I Want Decided'
Japan
Translated by Jane Hirshfield

Shikibu was a member of Japan's famed 'Thirty-six Medieval Poetry Immortals', a legendary collective of Japanese masters from antiquity. Here, Shikibu weaves two different kinds of absence – absence from the earth and the absence of desire. With this braid, she challenges readers to reflect upon which fate is truly worse.

Things I Want Decided

Which shouldn't exist
in his world,
the one who forgets
or the one
who is forgotten?

Which is better,
to love
one who has died
or not to see
each other when you're alive?

Which is better,
the distant lover
you long for
or the one you see daily
without desire?

Which is the least unreliable
among fickle things –
the swift rapids,
a flowing river,
or this human world?

Li Qingzhao
1084–*c.* 1155
'Late Spring'
China
Translated by Jiaosheng Wang

One of the great poets of China's Song Dynasty, Li Qingzhao
wrote some of the most immortal verse in the Chinese language.
Here she shows us that, in desperate longing, a person reaches out to
anything, anyone who might help. When they look out the window
and see even spring fading away, they might plea directly to the
god of spring.

Late Spring

The clepsydra has stopped dripping;
My dream is broken.
Heavy drinking last night
Intensifies my sorrow.
A chill falls on my jewelled pillow
As the kingfisher screen
Faces a new dawn.
Who swept away the fallen petals outside my door?
Was it the wind that blew the whole night through?

Echoes of a jade flute die away,
The player gone nobody knows where.
Spring, too, will soon be fled,
Yet he has the heart not to keep
His date to return.
I ask the God of Spring
Through the drifting clouds,
What I should do with this longing, this regret,
This moment of time.

Hildegard of Bingen
1098–1179
'Song to the Creator'
Germany
Translated by Barbara Newman

According to St Hildegard of Bingen, her poems came to her as visions directly from God. In her Scivias *she writes: 'I spoke and wrote these things not by the invention of my heart or that of any other person, but as by the secret mysteries of God I heard and received them in the heavenly places. And again I heard a voice from Heaven saying to me, "Cry out, therefore, and write thus!"'*

Song to the Creator

You, all-accomplishing
Word of the Father
are the light of primordial
daybreak over the spheres.
You, the foreknowing
mind of divinity,
foresaw all your works
as you willed them,
your prescience hidden
in the heart of your power,
your power like a wheel around the world,
whose circling never began
and never slides to an end.

Mahadeviyakka
Twelfth century
India
Translated by Jane Hirshfield

When I think about how to write mystery, unknowing, without
trying to resolve it, I think about this poem by the ancient
Kannada poet Mahadeviyakka, who some say was married to
the god Shiva. It seems that, for life's greatest questions, language
often fails even our species' greatest poets. Or, not 'fails', exactly,
but becomes almost beside the point. The exasperation in the
final line still makes me gasp.

I do not call it his sign,
I do not call it becoming one with his sign.
I do not call it union,
I do not call it harmony with union.
I do not say something has happened,
I do not say nothing has happened.
I will not name it You,
I will not name it I.
Now that the White Jasmine Lord is myself,
What use for words at all?

Attar of Nishapur
c. 1145–*c.* 1221
'Parable of the Dead Dervishes in the Desert'
Iran
Translated by Sholeh Wolpé

*Attar – a pen name that means 'apothecary' in Persian – was
one of the great early Sufi poets. Many speak of him largely for
his profound influence on Rūmī, but he was a major poet in his
own right. His* Conference of the Birds, *from which this excerpt is
taken, is one of the bedrocks of ancient Persian literature.*

Parable of the Dead Dervishes in the Desert

Disappear inside the Divine –
there you will find freedom.
There is nothing outside that unity.

Stop boasting. Shut up and lose yourself;
there is no greater honor
than losing the ego for love.

St Francis of Assisi
c. 1181–1226
'Canticle of the Sun'
Italy
Translated by Bill Barrett

One of the very first pieces of literature composed in the Italian language, Francis's 'Canticle of the Sun' is also known as 'Laudes Creaturarum', or 'In Praise of the Creatures'.

Canticle of the Sun

Most high, all powerful, all good Lord! All praise is yours,
all glory, all honour, and all blessing. To you, alone, Most High,
do they belong. No mortal lips are worthy to pronounce your
name.

Be praised, my Lord, through all your creatures, especially
through my lord Brother Sun, who brings the day; and you give
light through him. And he is beautiful and radiant in all his
splendor! Of you, Most High, he bears the likeness.

Be praised, my Lord, through Sister Moon and the stars; in the
heavens you have made them, precious and beautiful.

Be praised, my Lord, through Brothers Wind and Air, and clouds
and storms, and all the weather, through which you give your
creatures sustenance.

Be praised, My Lord, through Sister Water; she is very useful, and
humble, and precious, and pure.

Be praised, my Lord, through Brother Fire, through whom you
brighten the night. He is beautiful and cheerful, and powerful
and strong.

Be praised, my Lord, through our sister Mother Earth, who feeds
us and rules us, and produces various fruits with colored flowers
and herbs.

Be praised, my Lord, through those who forgive for love of you;
through those who endure sickness and trial. Happy those who
endure in peace, for by you, Most High, they will be crowned.

Be praised, my Lord, through our Sister Bodily Death, from whose embrace no living person can escape. Woe to those who die in mortal sin! Happy those she finds doing your most holy will. The second death can do no harm to them.

Praise and bless my Lord, and give thanks, and serve him with great humility.

Wumen Huikai
1183–1260
From *The Gateless Gate*
China
Translated by Kōun Yamada

*This major thirteenth-century text is commonly referred to in
English as* The Gateless Gate, *which is a misleading translation,
as two different characters are used in the original Chinese (*The
Gateless Barrier *might be more accurate). It's fitting that even the
title of this classic book of Zen koans stymies us – within it are
forty-eight different 'cases' meant to challenge, confuse, baffle and
deepen our minds and spirit.*

CASE 27: NOT MIND, NOT BUDDHA

Case: A monk asked Nansen in all earnestness, 'Is there any Dharma that has not been preached to the people?' Nansen said, 'There is.' The monk said, 'What is the Dharma which has never been preached to the people?' Nansen said, 'This isn't mind; this isn't Buddha; this isn't a thing.'

Mumon's Commentary: Nansen was merely asked a question, and he exhausted all his possessions at once and went reduced to nothing.

Verse:
Speaking too much degrades virtue,
No-words is truly effective;
Even though the great ocean should change,
It can never be communicated to you.

Rūmī
c. 1207–1273
'Lift Now the Lid of the Jar of Heaven'
Iran
Translated by Andrew Harvey

Rūmī, like many of his Sufi contemporaries, believed that physical intoxication might thin the partition between him and the divine. One can find parallels to this idea elsewhere in this anthology, including in the Mazatec shaman María Sabina's poetry from her sacred mushroom ceremonies.

Lift Now the Lid of the Jar of Heaven

Pour, cupbearer, the wine of the invisible,
The name and sign of what has no sign!
Pour it abundantly, it is you who enrich the soul;
Make the soul drunk, and give it wings!
Come again, always-fresh one, and teach
All our cupbearers their sacred art!
Be a spring jetting from a heart of stone!
Break the pitcher of soul and body!
Make joyful all lovers of wine!
Foment a restlessness in the heart
Of the one who thinks only of bread!
Bread's a mason of the body's prison,
Wine a rain for the garden of the soul.
I've tied the ends of the earth together,
Lift now the lid of the jar of heaven.
Close those eyes that see only faults,
Open those that contemplate the invisible
So no mosques or temples or idols remain,
So 'this' or 'that' is drowned in His fire.

Mechthild of Magdeburg
c. 1207–c. 1282
Germany
Translated by Jane Hirshfield

Mechthild of Magdeburg was an early Christian mystic – her poems were largely recordings of her visionary encounters with the Lord. The image of the honeybee at the heart of this little poem is crystalline, precise, unforgettable.

Of all that God has shown me
I can speak just the smallest word,
Nor more than a honeybee
Takes on his foot
From an overspilling jar.

Saadi Shirazi
1210–c. 1291
'The Grass Cried Out'
Iran

*Saadi is such an important poet in Iran that devotees of his work
still make the pilgrimage to visit his shrine in Shiraz, more than
700 years after his death. Here Saadi gives us a glimpse of how a
spiritual poem might also argue for more equitable life on earth.*

The Grass Cried Out

Discovering a bouquet of freshly cut roses
set in a vase with long grass, I asked,
'Why are these roses
set here among filthy weeds?'

The grass cried out:
'Quiet! Our presence
doesn't spoil their fragrance!
Maybe we don't smell as sweet as roses,
but we too grew inside God's garden.'

Thomas Aquinas
1225–1274
'Lost, All in Wonder'
Italy
Translated by Gerard Manley Hopkins

*In medieval bestiaries, the mother pelican was said to pierce her
own breast in order to feed her starving nestlings with her own
blood. Aquinas here takes that striking behaviour as a metaphor
for Christ, for the Eucharist. The pelican iconography, cemented
by this poem's adoption into liturgy by Pope Urban IV, persists
to this day – the Louisiana state flag features a mother pelican
piercing her own breast.*

Lost, All in Wonder

Godhead here in hiding, whom I do adore,
Masked by these bare shadows, shape and nothing more,
See, Lord, at thy service low lies here a heart
Lost, all lost in wonder at the God thou art.

Seeing, touching, tasting are in thee deceived:
How says trusty hearing? that shall be believed;
What God's Son has told me, take for truth I do;
Truth himself speaks truly or there's nothing true.

On the cross thy godhead made no sign to men,
Here thy very manhood steals from human ken:
Both are my confession, both are my belief,
And I pray the prayer of the dying thief.

I am not like Thomas, wounds I cannot see,
But can plainly call thee Lord and God as he;
Let me to a deeper faith daily nearer move,
Daily make me harder hope and dearer love.

O thou our reminder of Christ crucified,
Living Bread, the life of us for whom he died,
Lend this life to me then: feed and feast my mind,
There be thou the sweetness man was meant to find.

Bring the tender tale true of the Pelican;
Bathe me, Jesu Lord, in what thy bosom ran –
Blood whereof a single drop has power to win
All the world forgiveness of its world of sin.

Jesu, whom I look at shrouded here below,
I beseech thee send me what I thirst for so,
Some day to gaze on thee face to face in light
And be blest for ever with thy glory's sight.
Amen.

Moses de León
1250–1305
From *The Sepher Zohar*
Spain
Translation by Nurho de Manhar

Some ancient mystic texts, like the Kabbalah's Zohar, *sought to engage received mysteries – here, the text of the Hebrew Bible – by deepening, instead of resolving, their inscrutabilities.*

Rabbi Simeon's Analogies of The Divine Life in Man

As Rabbi Simeon ceased speaking the students rose up to depart, but ere they left he himself stood up and said: 'I have still a few further remarks to make before going, on two passages of scripture, which seemingly are somewhat contradictory in expression to each other. The first is, "The Lord thy God is a consuming fire" (Deuter iv. 24); the other is, "but ye that cleaved unto the Lord your God are alive every one of you this day". (Deuter. iv. 4.)

'If the Lord be a consuming fire as here stated, how could the children of Israel on becoming joined unto the Lord escape from being consumed, and continue to live? It has been explained how the Divine Being is a fire that consumes every other kind of fire, for there are flames of fire more intense in their nature than others. To this statement I wish to add a few supplementary remarks. Whoever wishes to understand the mystery of union with the Divine will do well to reflect and meditate upon the flame proceeding from a lighted candle or a burning coal, in which may be recognized two kinds of flame or light, one white and the other dark or bluish in colour. The white flame ascends upwards in a straight line, the dark or blue part of the flame being below it and forming its basis. Though these be conjoined together, the white flame is always seen clearly and distinctly, and of the two is the most valuable and precious.

From these observations we may gather somewhat of the occult meaning of the *thekheloth* (blue fringes) mentioned in scripture. The dark or blue flame is connected and conjoined with that above it, namely, the white, and also below it with the candle or coal in a state of combustion. It becomes sometimes red, whilst the superior white flame never varies in colour and remains invariably the same. Furthermore, it is noticeable that the dark or blue flame consumes and wastes the substance of the coal or candle whence it emanates, but the white pure light consumes nothing and never varies. Therefore, when Moses proclaims the Lord to be a consuming fire, he alludes to the astral fluid or flame that consumes everything similar to the dark flame that wastes and destroys the substance of the candle or coal. In using the term thy God, not our God, Moses refers to the white or Divine light which destroys nothing, in which he himself had been and came down from Mount Sinai out of it uninjured and intact. This is the case with everyone who lives in the Divine light of the higher life. He lives, then, the true or real life, and the astral light of the lower earthly life cannot harm or injure him. Therefore, to the children of Israel who had sanctified themselves and attained to this life, Moses could truly say: 'ye cleaved unto the Lord, your God, and are alive as at this time.' Above the white flame there is yet another arising out of it, yet unseen and unrecognizable by human sight and has reference to the greatest of mysteries, dim gleamings and notions of which are revealed to us by the different flames of a lighted candle or a burning coal.

As Rabbi Simeon ceased speaking, Rabbi Pinchus embraced him, exclaiming: 'The Lord be praised! the Merciful One, who has led me hither.' Rabbi Simeon, along with his students, went and accompanied Rabbi Pinchus on his journey for three leagues, and then bidding him adieu returned homewards.

Dante Alighieri
1265–1321
From *Inferno*, Canto III
Italy
Translated by Mary Jo Bang

T. S. Eliot famously wrote: 'Dante and Shakespeare divide the world between them. There is no third.' Jorge Luis Borges called The Divine Comedy *'the best book literature has ever achieved'. Few texts, save the Bible itself, have had a greater impact on European art.*

WELCOME TO THE CITY OF WOE.
WELCOME TO EVERLASTING SADNESS.
WELCOME TO THE GRAVE CAVE.

JUSTICE MADE THE MAKER BUILD IT JUST LIKE THIS,
WITH PRIMITIVE LOVE AND BRICKS OF WISDOM.
IF BEING IS POWER, POWER CREATED IT, I.E., IT IS.

BEFORE THIS, THERE WAS NOTHING THAT WASN'T
ETERNAL AND AFTER, NOTHING BUT THE ETERNAL.
YOU, WHO HAVE NO HOPE, ENTER HERE.

These words in soot and all in caps, as if
By a hurried hand, were scrawled on the stone overhead,
Above a creaking door. 'Sir,' I said, 'this is harsh.'

He spoke like an expert nephew to a drunkard uncle:
'Now you need to leave behind your fear.
Now you need to kill your cowardice.

We're where I said we'd come to,
The place where you'd see the wretched dead
Who have lost the aid of their intellect.'

He touched my hand as if to tell me all would be all right.
Then we crossed over from where we'd been
Into the inner sanctum that houses hidden things.

The starless air was echoing
With countless sighs, horrific cries.
Extended loud laments. I was in tears as I listened.

The angry accents, the strident utterances,
The striking hands, the near-deafening chorus
Of a million dolls' dark inner voices crying

'Ma-ma, ma-ma, ma-ma' veered off walls and swirled
Around and around, like sand in a storm
Becomes one with the wind that carries it.

And I, circled by horror, said, 'Sir,
What am I hearing? Who are these people
So overcome by grief?'

He said, 'This is the inheritance
Of the contemptible
Who did nothing wrong but nothing right.

They blend together with that band of vile angels
Who didn't rebel but who also didn't stand with God,
But only for themselves, in selfishness.

To preserve its beauty, Heaven threw them out.
Deepest Hell doesn't want them, since the truly wicked
Would be able to gloat, "We're worse,

We're truly depraved." I asked, 'What torments them?
Why do they cry so loud and so unremittingly?'
He answered: 'I'll tell you quickly.

They wish to die but cannot.
Their blind lives are so empty, so without reprieve,
They envy the nothing that an ending would be.

They're not meant to be remembered.
Mercy turns her back; justice disdains them.
They're not worth our attention. Look, and then let's go.'

I caught sight of a banner flitting about so restlessly
And moving forward so fast it seemed unable to take a stand.
It was followed by a sad and endless train

Of people racing after.
Never had I dreamed
Death had so many sycophants.

I saw some I recognized and then the ghost of one
Who'd stood down when faced with doing good,
And chose instead to be a coward.

I knew, incontestably, this scourge,
These despicable cowards, were the enemies
Of both Jekyll and Hyde.

They'd never lived and now would never die.
Naked as the day they were born,
Bitter wasps and hornets covered them.

Blood trickled between their tears;
This sorry sticky mixture dripped from their chins
To their feet and into the mouths of maggots.

Farther on, beyond these, I saw a crowd
Gathered on the bank of a wide river.
I asked my guide, 'Could you please tell me

Who these are and why they're waiting
With such eagerness to board the boat
I can barely make out in the distance?'

He told me, 'Hush, it will all be clear
When we reach the bank
Of the miserable River Acheron.'

I was afraid I'd annoyed him by asking,
So I stared at my feet
And stayed quiet until we reached the river.

Then, out of nowhere, there was an old man
With white hair, coming toward us in a boat,
Growling, 'Give it up, you scum-uncles.

You'll never see the sky again.
Like Red Rover I'm taking you over to the other side,
Where you'll eat and drink perpetual darkness.

Your naked asses will feel the furnace and the ice.
And you, with the beating heart,
Step away from the dead.' When I stood my ground

He said, 'You can't get to where you're going from here.
You need the dinghy marked 'P' for Purgatory.
That one leaves from a different pier.'

Virgil said, 'Charon, calm down.' We were standing
On the ramp. 'It's been decided where decisions are made.
His passport has a stamp. Now leave it alone.'

The hairy cheeks of the boatman,
King of the river rats, went slack.
His fire-eyes flared but he kept silent.

The weary and naked ones, however, went ashen,
And gritted their teeth as soon as they heard
His vicious speech. They cursed God, their parents,

The human race, the moment of their conception,
Their fathers' seed, the space between
Their mothers' legs, and the bed where they were made.

Then they moved as one, as if conjoined, sobbing
All the while, along the evil shore that awaits
Any and all who fail to fear God,

Where demon Charon, his eyes like hollow furnaces
Filled with fire, herds them together with a nod or beckons
With a bent finger, smacking the stragglers with his oar.

Fall signals the tree to drop its leaves, and it does,
One after the other, until the branch looks down
And sees a blanket on the ground;

Like that, Adam's wicked children leave the shore
One by one when summoned,
The way trained birds come when called with a tin whistle,

Then they go, over the murky water.
Before the boat has landed on the far side,
A new group is already huddled naked on the near.

'Now,' said my teacher, 'to your earlier question:
The ones you see here have died before making amends.
They come from every known country.

The reason they're so eager to cross the river
Is that the desire for divine justice prompts them;
The very thing they fear is precisely what they want.

The good never board the boat –
So if Charon curses both your shoes, and the dirt
Beneath your feet, perhaps you now know why.'

At that, the pitch-dark plain shook.
Every aspect of that moment is burned into my brain:
The cold sweat inside my clothes,

The hot wind that rose off the ground wet with tears,
The massive crimson camera flash that lit the night scene
And turned us red. I lost it and dropped

Like someone seized by narcoleptic sleep.

From the *Sundiata*
1285 CE
Mali
Translated by David Conrad

The *Sundiata* is an epic poem of Mali that follows the hero
Sundiata Keita through great political and cosmic battles.
The epic orbits an eternal conflict between constructive and
destructive forces.

The Frenchmen asked my father (Naamu)
If he could say anything about how Paris was built. (Naamu)
My father said, "Yes, I can say something. (Na-amu)
The history of Paris." (Naamu)
My father said, (Naamu)
"The Paris you ask about, (Naamu)
It was not built by Frenchmen! (Naamu)
It was not built by Americans! (Na-amu)
It was not built by the English! (Naamuu)
It was not built by the Russians! (Naamu)
None of them built it. (Naamu)
They only saw it appear. (Naamuu)
Because they only saw it appear, they called it Paris." (Naamu)
(You heard it?) (Na-amu)
If Paris was ever built by anyone, it was God. (Naamu, true, naamu)
(I say this to you.) (Na-amu)
Do not be too concerned with blackness, (Naamu)
Do not be too concerned with whiteness, (Naamu)
Be more concerned with humanity. (Naamuu)
We are all equal. (Na-amu)
We all have life. (Naaaam')
We all go to sleep. (Naamu)
We all eat food. (Na-amu)
We all suckle breasts. (Naamu)
If you have come, you have come to your father's home. (Naamu)

> *[In an omitted passage, Sunjata accepts the leadership of
> Manden, and an elaborate series of sacrifices is performed
> in preparation for war against Soso.]*

Hafez
c. 1325–c. 1390
Ghazal 17
Iran
Translated by Charles Upton

'Hafez' was a pen name that literally meant 'the memorizer', but many of his poems embrace bewilderment and unknowing. What does Hafez say here is the great prize for a life spent in pursuit of the divine? 'Some day the Beloved will lift for you / A corner of the veil.'

The morning blossoms, and immediately the cloud conceals it
    under her veil.
The cup of the morning, my friends!
The morning cup!

The face of the tulip is withered
In the grip of the frost – wine, my friends!
Bring wine!

From the meadow the breeze of Paradise is blowing,
So drink pure wine – without pause, without end.

The rose has set her emerald throne in the centre of the meadow –
Bring wine red as ruby, wine red as fire!

The tavern door, again they've closed it –
Open it for us, you Opener of Doors!
It's amazing how quickly they rush to close it,
And always at a time like this!

Your ruby lip holds the rights of salt
Against those whose wounded hearts
Are roasted on a spit;

Let the ascetic drink wine like the reveller;
Let the wise fear God.
If your quest is for the water of life
Then drink sweet wine to the sound of the harp;

If you boldly seek for life like Alexander,
Then take as your trophy
The crimson lip of the
Beloved.

To the memory of the Saki, formed like the
youths of Paradise
Drink pure wine in the season of the rose.

Don't grieve, Hafez; your fortune has been told:
Some day the Beloved will lift for you
A corner of the veil.

Yaqui people
Date unknown
'Deer Song'
Meso-America
Translated by Larry Evers and Felipe S. Molina

*Reverent watching, reverent attention can, in the hands of
the right poet, elevate something to the realm of the divine.
This song, from the indigenous Yaqui tribe of Mexico and the
American Southwest, models that watching, and models radical
interdependence too, as the final lines compress the 'he' and the
'I' into one.*

Deer Song

There he comes out,
   there from the enchanted house,
      I come out from there.
There he comes out,
   there from the enchanted house,
      I come out from there.

There he comes out,
   there from the enchanted house,
      I come out from there.
There he comes out,
   there from the enchanted house,
      I come out from there.

Over there, I, in Yevuku Yoleme's
   flower-covered, flower patio,
      I have sparsely flowered antlers.
There he comes out,
   there from the enchanted house,
      I come out from there.

Nezahualcoyotl
1402–1472
'The Painted Book'
Mesoamerica
Translated by Miguel León-Portilla

*Nezahualcoyotl's name literally translates to 'the coyote who
fasts'. The ancient leader reminds me a bit of King David – he
was a great ruler, governing the state of Texcoco in present-day
Mexico, but he was also a philosopher, a warrior and a striking
poet. Like all great poets, Nezahualcoyotl constantly surprises,
subverts our expectations. Hearts full of paint! Flowers that write!*

1

In the house of paintings
the singing begins,
song is intoned,
flowers are spread,
the song rejoices.

Above the flowers is singing
the radiant pheasant:
his song expands
into the interior of the waters.
To him reply
all manner of red birds:
the dazzling red bird
sings a beautiful chant.

Your heart is a book of paintings,
You have come to sing,
to make Your drums resound.
You are the singer.
Within the house of springtime,
You make the people happy.

You alone bestow
intoxicating flowers,
precious flowers.
You are the singer.
Within the house of springtime,
You make the people happy.

2

With flowers You write,
O Giver of Life:
with songs You give color,
with songs You shade
those who must live on the earth.

Later You will destroy eagles and ocelots:
we live only in Your book of paintings,
here, on the earth.

With black ink You will blot out
all that was friendship,
brotherhood, nobility.

You give shading
to those who must live on the earth.
We live only in Your book of paintings,
here on the earth.

Kabir
1440–1518
India
Translated by Arvind Krishna Mehrotra

The poet Kabir was counted as a saint by both Brahmans and
Muslim communities. His poetry celebrated oneness, wonder and
mystery; all three themes are abundantly present in this short
piece.

Brother, I've seen some
  Astonishing sights:
A lion keeping watch
  Over pasturing cows;
A mother delivered
  After her son was;
A guru prostrated
  Before his disciple;
Fish spawning
  On treetops;
A cat carrying away
  A dog;
A gunny-sack
  Driving a bullock-cart;
A buffalo going out to graze,
  Sitting on a horse;
A tree with its branches in the earth,
  Its roots in the sky;
A tree with flowering roots.

This verse, says Kabir,
  Is your key to the universe.
If you can figure it out.

Mirabai
c. 1498–c. 1547
India
Translated by Jane Hirshfield

So many poets seek the divine by looking toward nature or up at the heavens. Here, the Bhakti saint and Hindu mystic poet Mirabai shows how the divine might be discovered internally, facing our 'inmost chamber'.

O friend, understand: the body
is like the ocean,
rich with hidden treasures.

Open your inmost chamber and light its lamp.

Within the body are gardens,
rare flowers, peacocks, the inner Music;
within the body a lake of bliss,
on it the white soul-swans take their joy.

And in the body, a vast market –
go there, trade,
sell yourself for a profit you can't spend.

Mira says, her Lord is beyond praising.
Allow her to dwell near Your feet.

Yoruba people
1500
From *A Recitation of Ifa*
Yorubaland
Translated by Awotunde Aworine, John Olaniyi Ogundipe and
Judith Gleason

*A system of prophesy and also a religion in itself, Ifa has
been practised by Yoruba people – and others – for centuries.
Ifa divination draws from a literary corpus known as* odu *to
interpret an individual's future, or help gain insights regarding
major life decisions. This text is merely one sample generated
using ancient Ifa divination techniques.*

Greetings for the sacrifice!
Now let us praise Ika Meji –
Can you see how Ifa came to this designation?
Up against the wall's no place
    to extend 'long life!' to your elders;
Coming straight on,
    gazing vaguely away
    signifies a voracious visitor;
Might look as though I were up to no good,
    followed by all of you; stay home,
    said the snake to his hungry children

Made Ifa for Slim-pickings,
    stubby little fellow who will survive
    twenty thousand years in this world
    if he sacrifice
    ten pigeons, a scroungy cock, and ten bags of cowries.
He sacrificed, they made Ifa leaves for him,
    and he did not die –
    unlike the broom swept into a wisp,
    he stayed together
We have sacrificed efficaciously.

Now let's get on to row two:
King of the counting house
don't count me
Turn around, misery,
count me out;
Snake-eyes,
if we're being counted,

why'd ya call me?
Accountable for no-account?
No one's seen me sin;
no wickedness on me.
Mother counts the baskets
Father counts the bins
One by one they counted us down,
but we fixed them.
Ifa, hearing this:
How is it all of you who live
in this rickety town
have icky names?
'Cause hicks are what we called ourselves
till you hit the scene.
So that's the reason, Ifa said,
All your lives you've been higgledy-piggledy, sick, sick, sick,
like housewives rushing before the storm
picking laundry off limbs.
Now go distribute money to snails,
for it's their shells that spiral in –
like Mother Yemoja making medicine
with viper's head. You dig?
She covered herself with prickly cloth;
and when this hedgehog edged over to sit
beside her victim, they said:
Go feed grass to *that* horse
standing by the corn bin.
When hedgehog hit
it was beancake-vendor
fell down dead.
Now snail turned gravedigger;
viper mourned the death
of beancake-vendor.

Creeping snail upon snail
adds insult to injury;
If witch's snare can't smell the entrance,
snail within will survive forever.
Will dog bite the heel of bush cow?
Never! We sneaked out of the way
to our rickety town
early in the morning.

Trading for years and nothing to show for it
    called on
Axe strikes tree, definitively,
    diviner of the house of Orunmila.
Secret arrived on foot,
    blessed the rackety-packety inhabitants of Ika;
and when he had done,
we praised the diviner, saying:
Secret said I will have money,
    and here is money.
Axe strikes tree, definitively,
    as blade's edge
    is the tongue of secrets.
Diviner says I will have a wife –
    Here she is.
Axe strikes tree
    Power sits
    in the mouth
    of Ifa
Diviner says I will have offspring –
    Here are children.
    His tongue speaks
    with authority:
Diviner says I will build me a house –

See, over there –
Secret's spit is commanding.
Diviner says I will see good things –
    There they are, everywhere, everything –
    Energy fills the speech of diviner.
Then he started singing:

Spiky fingers	*grip iniquity*
Aka leaves	*bind hands of mine enemy*

Reverse wickedness!

Close their hands	*globe, peel, pound, knead*

Till there's no remainder!
May they die young!

Spiny cloth	*slim leaves*
bend and twist	*till there be*
no vise in	*hostility*

So be it!

Greetings! May our sacrifice see us through this thicket.

Teresa of Ávila
1515–1582
'Laughter Came from Every Brick'
Spain
Translated by Daniel Ladinsky

*A wealthy noblewoman who gave up all her riches for life in
a convent, Teresa of Ávila eventually became one of the great
Christian mystics of her age. I find myself so moved by the
juxtaposition of joy and burden in this poem, the suffering of the
crucifix set against the pleasure of divine love.*

Laughter Came from Every Brick

Just these two words He spoke
changed my life,
'Enjoy Me'.
What a burden I thought I was to carry –
a crucifix, as did He.
Love once said to me, 'I know a song,
would you like to hear it?'
And laughter came from every brick in the street
and from every pore
in the sky.
After a night of prayer, He
changed my life when
He sang,
'Enjoy Me'.

Gaspara Stampa
1523–1554
'Deeply repentant of my sinful ways'
Italy
Translated by Lorna de Lucci

Though she died young, Gaspara Stampa wrote 311 poems and became one of the greatest poets of the Renaissance. Rainer Maria Rilke, another poet in this volume, evokes Stampa in his first Duino Elegy.

Deeply repentant of my sinful ways

Deeply repentant of my sinful ways
And of my trivial, manifold desires,
Of squandering, alas, these few brief days
Of fugitive life in tending love's vain fires,
To Thee, Lord, Who dost move hard hearts again,
And render warmth unto the frozen snow,
And lighten every bitter load of pain
For those who with Thy sacred ardours glow,
    To Thee I turn, O stretch forth Thy right hand
And from this whirlpool rescue me, for I
Without Thine aid could never reach the land;
O willingly for us didst suffer loss,
And to redeem mankind hung on the Cross,
O gentle Saviour, leave me not to die.

St John of the Cross
1542–1591
Spain
Translated by Antonio de Nicolás

Few poets capture the fevered, desperate longing to commune with an invisible divine more movingly than St John of the Cross, who was born Juan de Yepes y Álvarez and was a friend of Teresa of Ávila. Much of St John of the Cross's greatest poetry, including this piece, was written under duress while being held prisoner (and tortured) by a group of Carmelite monks.

O Love's living flame,
Tenderly you wound
My soul's deepest centre!
Since you no longer evade me,
Will you, please, at last conclude:
Rend the veil of this sweet encounter!

O cautery so tender!
O pampered wound!
O soft hand! O touch so delicately strange,
Tasting of eternal life
And cancelling all debts!
Killing, death into life you change!

O lamps of fiery lure,
In whose shining transparence
The deep cavern of the senses,
Blind and obscure,
Warmth and light, with strange flares,
Gives with the lover's caresses!

How tame and loving
Your memory rises in my breast,
Where secretly only you live,
And in your fragrant breathing,
Full of goodness and grace,
How delicately in love you make me feel!

Mayan people
1550
From the *Popol Vuh* (*The Vision of the First Men*)
Meso-America
Translated by Michael Bazzett

*This Mayan creation story was transmitted orally throughout
Meso-America for centuries. It wasn't until 1703 when a
Dominican monk named Francisco Ximénez translated it into
Spanish that the* Popol Vuh *started to be read and shared by
European audiences.*

It is said these men were
simply framed and shaped:

they had no mother,
they had no father.

They were merely lone men.
No woman gave them birth.

Nor were they borne
by the Framer and the Shaper,

by She who has borne children,
and He who has planted them.

It was simply the pure spirit
and glinting spark of insight

of the Framer and the Shaper,
of Sovereign and Quetzal Serpent,

of She who has borne children,
and He who has planted them,

that framed and gave them shape.
They looked like true people,

and true people they became.
They spoke and they conversed.

They looked and they listened.
They walked and they grasped things,
and they held them in their hands.

They were excellent people,
well made and handsome.

They appeared with manly faces
and began to breathe,
and so they became,

and they looked around them,
their vision coming all at once:

their sight was completed
by the world around them,

their knowledge was completed
by everything beneath the sky.

When they gazed about them,
the looked intently and deeply
into the womb of the sky and earth.

It took less than a moment to take it in.
In that brief time, they saw everything.

They had not yet taken a step,
when they already knew the world:

everything beneath the sky
was seen from where they looked,
and their knowledge was crowded full.

Their vision passed beyond the trees,
beyond the rocks and lakes and seas,
beyond the mountains and the valleys.

They were truly honoured people,
Balam Quitze and Balam Acab,
Mahucutah and Iqui Balam.

Christopher Marlowe
1564–1593
From *Faustus*
England

From the Elizabethan playwright Christopher Marlowe we get the tragedy of Dr Faustus, a scholar who sells his soul for all the knowledge of the cosmos. Once he has it, however, he uses it for mostly silly things – he becomes invisible in order to bop the Pope on the ears and conjures up Helen of Troy for a kiss.

FAUSTUS: Ah, Faustus,
Now hast thou but one bare hour to live,
And then thou must be damn'd perpetually!
Stand still, you ever-moving spheres of heaven,
That time may cease, and midnight never come;
Fair Nature's eye, rise, rise again, and make
Perpetual day; or let this hour be but
A year, a month, a week, a natural day,
That Faustus may repent and save his soul!
O lente, lente currite, noctis equi!
The stars move still, time runs, the clock will strike,
The devil will come, and Faustus must be damn'd.
O, I'll leap up to my God! – Who pulls me down? –
See, see, where Christ's blood streams in the firmament!
One drop would save my soul, half a drop: ah, my Christ! –
Ah, rend not my heart for naming of my Christ!
Yet will I call on him: O, spare me, Lucifer! –
Where is it now? 'tis gone: and see, where God
Stretcheth out his arm, and bends his ireful brows!
Mountains and hills, come, come, and fall on me,
And hide me from the heavy wrath of God!
No, no!
Then will I headlong run into the earth:
Earth, gape! O, no, it will not harbour me!
You stars that reign'd at my nativity,
Whose influence hath allotted death and hell,
Now draw up Faustus, like a foggy mist.
Into the entrails of yon labouring cloud[s],
That, when you vomit forth into the air,
My limbs may issue from your smoky mouths,
So that my soul may but ascend to heaven!

[The clock strikes the half-hour.]
Ah, half the hour is past! 'twill all be past anon
O God,
If thou wilt not have mercy on my soul,
Yet for Christ's sake, whose blood hath ransom'd me,
Impose some end to my incessant pain;
Let Faustus live in hell a thousand years,
A hundred thousand, and at last be sav'd!
O, no end is limited to damned souls!
Why wert thou not a creature wanting soul?
Or why is this immortal that thou hast?
Ah, Pythagoras' metempsychosis, were that true,
This soul should fly from me, and I be chang'd
Unto some brutish beast! all beasts are happy,
For, when they die,
Their souls are soon dissolv'd in elements;
But mine must live still to be plagu'd in hell.
Curs'd be the parents that engender'd me!
No, Faustus, curse thyself, curse Lucifer
That hath depriv'd thee of the joys of heaven.
[The clock strikes twelve.]
O, it strikes, it strikes! Now, body, turn to air,
Or Lucifer will bear thee quick to hell!
[Thunder and lightning.]
O soul, be chang'd into little water-drops,
And fall into the ocean, ne'er be found!
[Enter DEVILS.]
My God, my god, look not so fierce on me!
Adders and serpents, let me breathe a while!
Ugly hell, gape not! come not, Lucifer!
I'll burn my books! – Ah, Mephistopheles!
[Exeunt DEVILS with FAUSTUS.]

William Shakespeare
1564–1616
Sonnet 146
England

In Sonnet 146, Shakespeare presents an argument for trading lavish finery for internal spiritual wealth – 'Within be fed, without be rich no more.' Though Shakespeare himself was comfortably well off for most of his life, the magisterial celebration of self-restraint in his sonnet connects it with some of the other more ascetic texts collected in this volume.

Sonnet 146

Poor soul, the centre of my sinful earth,
... these rebel powers that thee array,
Why dost thou pine within and suffer dearth,
Painting thy outward walls so costly gay?
Why so large cost, having so short a lease,
Dost thou upon thy fading mansion spend?
Shall worms, inheritors of this excess,
Eat up thy charge? Is this thy body's end?
Then, soul, live thou upon thy servant's loss,
And let that pine to aggravate thy store;
Buy terms divine in selling hours of dross;
Within be fed, without be rich no more.
  So shalt thou feed on death, that feeds on men,
  And death once dead, there's no more dying then.

John Donne
1572–1631
'Batter my heart, three-person'd God'
England

Donne, the greatest of the Metaphysical poets, wrote to God
like a lover – romantically, as in 'dearly I love you', and also
erotically, 'Batter my heart', 'you ravish me'. To hear this in 2022
still feels radical, subversive – what must it have felt like to his
contemporary readers, coming from a cleric of the Anglican
Church? Donne must have feared such a reception – he never
published many of his more embodied poems, though they were
passed around surreptitiously between friends and fans.

Batter my heart, three-person'd God

Batter my heart, three-person'd God, for you
As yet but knock, breathe, shine, and seek to mend;
That I may rise and stand, o'erthrow me, and bend
Your force to break, blow, burn, and make me new.
I, like an usurp'd town to another due,
Labour to admit you, but oh, to no end;
Reason, your viceroy in me, me should defend,
But is captiv'd, and proves weak or untrue.
Yet dearly I love you, and would be lov'd fain,
But am betroth'd unto your enemy;
Divorce me, untie or break that knot again,
Take me to you, imprison me, for I,
Except you enthrall me, never shall be free,
Nor ever chaste, except you ravish me.

Nahuatl people
Sixteenth century
'The Midwife Addresses the Woman'
Meso-America
Translated by John Bierhorst

*This early Meso-American poem of the Nahuatl people –
indigenous groups located primarily in present-day Central
America – depicts a stark juxtaposition between heavenly
life and life on earth. It's also possible to map the 'five stages
of grief' – denial, anger, bargaining, depression, acceptance –
directly on to this poem, which preceded the formal scientific
introduction of this model by 500 years.*

The Midwife Addresses the Woman

Precious feather, child,
Eagle woman, dear one,
Dove, daring daughter,
You have laboured, you have toiled,
Your task is finished.
You came to the aid of your Mother, the noble lady, Cihuacoatl
    Quilaztli.
You received, raised up, and held the shield, the little buckler that
    she laid in your hands: she your Mother, the noble lady,
    Cihuacoatl Quilaztli.
Now wake! Rise! Stand up!
Comes the daylight, the daybreak:
Dawn's house has risen crimson, it comes up standing.
The crimson swifts, the crimson swallows, sing,
And all the crimson swans are calling.
Get up, stand up! Dress yourself!
Go! Go seek the good place, the perfect place, the home of your
    Mother,
your Father, the Sun,
The place of happiness, joy,
Delight, rejoicing.
Go! Go follow your Mother, your Father, the Sun.
May his elder sisters bring you to him: they the exalted, the
    celestial women,
who always and forever know happiness, joy, delight, and
    rejoicing, in the company and in the presence of our
    Mother, our Father, the Sun; who make him happy with
    their shouting.
My child, darling daughter, lady,
You spent yourself, you laboured manfully:

You made yourself a victor, a warrior for Our Lord, though
	not without consuming all your strength; you sacrificed
	yourself.
Yet you earned a compensation, a reward: a good, perfect,
	precious death.
By no means did you die in vain.
And are you truly dead? You have made a sacrifice. Yet how else
	could you have become worthy of what you now deserve?
You will live forever, you will be happy, you will rejoice in the
	company and in the presence of our holy ones, the exalted
	women. Farewell, my daughter, my child. Go be with them,
	join them. Let them hold you and take you in.
May you join them as they cheer him and shout to him: our
	Mother, our Father, the Sun;
And may you be with them always, whenever they go in their
	rejoicing.

But my little child, my daughter, my lady,
You went away and left us, you deserted us, and we are but old
	men and old women.
You have cast aside your mother and your father.
Was this your wish? No, you were summoned, you were called.
Yet without you, how can we survive?
How painful will it be, this hard old age?
Down what alleys or in what doorways will we perish?
Dear lady, do not forget us! Remember the hardships that we see,
	that we suffer, here on earth:
The heat of the sun presses against us; also the wind, icy and cold:
This flesh, this clay of ours, is starved and trembling.
And we, poor prisoners of our stomachs!
There is nothing we can do.
Remember us, my precious daughter, O eagle woman, O lady!
You lie beyond in happiness. In the good place, the perfect place,

You live.
In the company and in the presence of our lord,
You live.
You as living flesh can see him, you as living flesh can call to him.
Pray to him for us!
Call to him for us!
This is the end,
We leave the rest to you.

George Herbert
1593–1633
'Easter Wings'
England

The wings the great Metaphysical poet George Herbert writes about actually appear here on the page. And while the visual pyrotechnics were certainly innovative, it's Herbert's language, the symmetry – 'Affliction shall advance the flight in me' – that makes his poem timeless.

Easter Wings

Lord, who createdst man in wealth and store,
  Though foolishly he lost the same,
    Decaying more and more,
      Till he became
       Most poore:
       With thee
      O let me rise
    As larks, harmoniously,
  And sing this day thy victories:
Then shall the fall further the flight in me.

My tender age in sorrow did beginne
  And still with sicknesses and shame.
    Thou didst so punish sinne,
      That I became
       Most thinne.
       With thee
      Let me combine,
    And feel thy victorie:
  For, if I imp my wing on thine,
Affliction shall advance the flight in me.

Walatta Petros/Gälawdewos
Seventeenth century
From *The Life and Struggles of Our Mother Walatta Petros*
Ethiopia
Translated by Wendy Laura Belcher and Michael Kleiner

This seventeenth-century hagiography of the Ethiopian saint Walatta Petros is the earliest known book-length biography of an African woman, unavailable in English translation until 2015.

Chapter 65: Our Mother Drives Demons
Away from a Royal Woman

Now we will further tell you about our holy mother Walatta Petros's great, awe-inspiring power: how the demons feared and fled her. One day, a great lady from among those of royal blood came to our holy mother Walatta Petros to pay her a visit. The princess met with Walatta Petros, sat down in front of her, and the two of them conversed with each other for some time. Then our blessed mother Walatta Petros raised her eyes and saw demons amusing themselves with the princess and surrounding her entire body, like flies and mosquitoes surround a rotting carcass. When our holy mother Walatta Petros looked straight at the demons, they became terrified and took flight. Yet when she lowered [her eyes] to the ground again, they instantly swarmed back and surrounded the princess as before. But when Walatta Petros again looked at them, they [again] took flight.

After the woman had left, Ghirmana asked Walatta Petros about this matter because she had been with them. Ghirmana said to Walatta Petros, 'Please tell me what you have seen over that woman, because I saw you raising your eyes once and looking toward her, but then casting them down to the ground in embarrassment. Therefore, I have come to suspect that you noticed something.'

Our blessed mother Walatta Petros indignantly replied to her, 'What type of thought rises in your heart? I have seen nothing whatsoever over her!' Yet, Ghirmana again implored her. So Walatta Petros then told her that she had seen demons, as we described earlier.

My loved ones, do you see how the demons feared our holy mother Walatta Petros and took flight from her? Truly, this recalls the saying of the Spiritual Elder, 'Just as jackals become scared and hide at the roar of the lion, so the word of the sage frightens the evil spirits' and puts them to flight.'

John Milton
1608–1674
From *Paradise Lost*, Book 4
England

Among the enduring contributions of Milton's Paradise Lost
*are the unrhymed line (Milton called rhyme 'the invention of a
barbarous age'), a heliocentric universe (a young Milton once
met Galileo, by then blind and under house arrest in Florence),
and new additions to the English dictionary still in use today
including 'fragrance', 'stunning' and, of course, 'satanic'.*

O, for that warning voice, which he, who saw
The Apocalypse, heard cry in Heaven aloud,
Then when the Dragon, put to second rout,
Came furious down to be revenged on men,
Woe to the inhabitants on earth! that now,
While time was, our first parents had been warned
The coming of their secret foe, and 'scaped,
Haply so 'scaped his mortal snare: For now
Satan, now first inflamed with rage, came down,
The tempter ere the accuser of mankind,
To wreak on innocent frail Man his loss
Of that first battle, and his flight to Hell:
Yet, not rejoicing in his speed, though bold
Far off and fearless, nor with cause to boast,
Begins his dire attempt; which nigh the birth
Now rolling boils in his tumultuous breast,
And like a devilish engine back recoils
Upon himself; horrour and doubt distract
His troubled thoughts, and from the bottom stir
The Hell within him; for within him Hell
He brings, and round about him, nor from Hell
One step, no more than from himself, can fly
By change of place: Now conscience wakes despair,
That slumbered; wakes the bitter memory
Of what he was, what is, and what must be
Worse; of worse deeds worse sufferings must ensue.
Sometimes towards Eden, which now in his view
Lay pleasant, his grieved look he fixes sad;
Sometimes towards Heaven, and the full-blazing sun,
Which now sat high in his meridian tower:
Then, much revolving, thus in sighs began.

O thou, that, with surpassing glory crowned,
Lookest from thy sole dominion like the God
Of this new world; at whose sight all the stars
Hide their diminished heads; to thee I call,
But with no friendly voice, and add thy name,
O Sun! to tell thee how I hate thy beams,
That bring to my remembrance from what state
I fell, how glorious once above thy sphere;
Till pride and worse ambition threw me down
Warring in Heaven against Heaven's matchless King:
Ah, wherefore! he deserved no such return
From me, whom he created what I was
In that bright eminence, and with his good
Upbraided none; nor was his service hard.
What could be less than to afford him praise,
The easiest recompense, and pay him thanks,
How due! yet all his good proved ill in me,
And wrought but malice; lifted up so high
I 'sdeined subjection, and thought one step higher
Would set me highest, and in a moment quit
The debt immense of endless gratitude,
So burdensome still paying, still to owe,
Forgetful what from him I still received,
And understood not that a grateful mind
By owing owes not, but still pays, at once
Indebted and discharged; what burden then
O, had his powerful destiny ordained
Me some inferiour Angel, I had stood
Then happy; no unbounded hope had raised
Ambition! Yet why not some other Power
As great might have aspired, and me, though mean,
Drawn to his part; but other Powers as great
Fell not, but stand unshaken, from within

Or from without, to all temptations armed.
Hadst thou the same free will and power to stand?
Thou hadst: whom hast thou then or what to accuse,
But Heaven's free love dealt equally to all?
Be then his love accursed, since love or hate,
To me alike, it deals eternal woe.
Nay, cursed be thou; since against his thy will
Chose freely what it now so justly rues.
Me miserable! which way shall I fly
Infinite wrath, and infinite despair?
Which way I fly is Hell; myself am Hell;
And, in the lowest deep, a lower deep
Still threatening to devour me opens wide,
To which the Hell I suffer seems a Heaven.
O, then, at last relent: Is there no place
Left for repentance, none for pardon left?
None left but by submission; and that word
Disdain forbids me, and my dread of shame
Among the Spirits beneath, whom I seduced
With other promises and other vaunts
Than to submit, boasting I could subdue
The Omnipotent. Ay me! they little know
How dearly I abide that boast so vain,
Under what torments inwardly I groan,
While they adore me on the throne of Hell.
With diadem and scepter high advanced,
The lower still I fall, only supreme
In misery: Such joy ambition finds.
But say I could repent, and could obtain,
By act of grace, my former state; how soon
Would highth recall high thoughts, how soon unsay
What feigned submission swore? Ease would recant
Vows made in pain, as violent and void.

For never can true reconcilement grow,
Where wounds of deadly hate have pierced so deep:
Which would but lead me to a worse relapse
And heavier fall: so should I purchase dear
Short intermission bought with double smart.
This knows my Punisher; therefore as far
From granting he, as I from begging, peace;
All hope excluded thus, behold, in stead
Of us out-cast, exil'd, his new delight,
Mankind created, and for him this world.
So farewell, hope; and with hope farewell, fear;
Farewell, remorse! all good to me is lost;
Evil, be thou my good; by thee at least
Divided empire with Heaven's King I hold,
By thee, and more than half perhaps will reign;
As Man ere long, and this new world, shall know.

Bashō
1644–1694
'Death Song' and 'In Kyoto'
Japan
'In Kyoto' translated by Jane Hirshfield

*Matsuo Bashō is one of Japan's haiku masters. 'Death Song',
his final poem, was purportedly written in the moments
before his death.*

In Kyoto,
hearing the cuckoo,
I long for Kyoto.

Death-sick on my journey
My dreams run out ahead of me
Across the empty field

Juana Inés de la Cruz
1648–1695
'Suspend singer swan'
Mexico
Translated by Michael Smith

The early Mexican philosopher-poet Juana Inés de la Cruz
composed in Latin, Nahuatl and Spanish. Though she lived most
of her life as a nun, she wrote passionately in support of women's
rights and against Spanish colonialism.

Suspend singer swan

Suspend, singer swan, the sweet strain:
see how the lord that Delphi sees
exchanges for you the gentle lyre for pipe
and to Admetus makes a pastoral sound.

As gentle song, though strong, moved
stones and tamed the wrath of hell,
so it retreats, abashed, when you are heard:
your instrument blames the church itself.

For though the works of ancient builders
cannot match its columns,
nothing's greater than your song

when your clear voice strikes its stones,
and your sweet tones surpass it,
dwarf it, while making it grow the more.

Yosa Buson
1716–1784
Japan
Translated by Allan Persinger

*A contemporary of Bashō and Issa, Yosa Buson was a Japanese
painter and poet. As with most of the poet's work, these poems
are made of few words, but their real subject – the true divine
being courted – seems often to be stillness; language is just a cast
moulded over the silence we are really meant to be hearing.*

1.

A solitude
even greater than last year's –
autumn ending.

2.

Looking at flowers
while treading on them in sandals
a sleepy morning

3.

The worthless monk
is beating his worthless
iron begging bowl

Olaudah Equiano
c. 1745–1797
'Miscellaneous Verses'
Kingdom of Benin, America, England

*Equiano was a formerly enslaved person who was eventually able
to purchase his freedom and spend his later years devoted to the
Church and abolitionist causes. He wrote staggering narratives
around the myriad atrocities of slavery, then braided them into
odes to the grandeur and sanctuary of God.*

Miscellaneous Verses

Well may I say my life has been
One scene of sorrow and of pain;
From early days I griefs have known,
And as I grew my griefs have grown.

Dangers were always in my path
And fear of wrath and sometimes death;
While pale dejection in me reigned
I often wept, by grief constrained.

When taken from my native land
By an unjust and cruel band,
How did uncommon dread prevail!
My sighs no more I could conceal.

To ease my mind I often strove,
And tried my trouble to remove;
I sung and uttered sighs between,
Assayed to stifle guilt with sin.

But oh! not all that I could do
Would stop the current of my woe;
Conviction still my vileness showed –
How great my guilt, how lost to good.

Prevented that I could not die,
Nor could to one sure refuge fly;
An orphan state I had to mourn,
Forsook by all and left forlorn.

Those who beheld my downcast mien
Could not guess at my woes unseen;
They by appearance could not know
The troubles that I waded through.

Lust, anger, blasphemy and pride
With legions of such ills beside
Troubled my thoughts, while doubts and fears
Clouded and darkened most my years.

Sighs now no more would be confined,
They breathed the trouble of my mind;
I wished for death but checked the word,
And often prayed unto the Lord.

Unhappy, more than some on earth,
I thought the place that gave me birth
Strange thoughts oppressed, while I replied,
'Why not in Ethiopia died?'

And why thus spared when nigh to hell?
God only knew, I could not tell!
A tottering fence, a bowing wall
I thought myself e'er since the fall.

Ofttimes I mused and nigh despair,
While birds melodious filled the air –
Thrice happy songsters, ever free,
How blest were they compared to me!

Thus all things added to my pain
While grief compelled me to complain;
When sable clouds began to rise,
My mind grew darker than the skies.

The English nation called to leave,
How did my breast with sorrows heave!
I longed for rest, cried 'Help me, Lord –
Some mitigation, Lord, afford!'

Yet on dejected still I went,
Heart-throbbing woes within me pent;
Nor land nor sea could comfort give,
Nor aught my anxious mind relieve.

Weary with troubles yet unknown
To all but God and self alone,
Numerous months for peace I strove,
Numerous foes I had to prove.

Inured to dangers, grief and woes,
Trained up midst perils, death and foes,
I said, 'Must it thus ever be?
No quiet is permitted me.'

Hard hap and more than heavy lot!
I prayed to God, 'Forget me not;
What thou ordain'st help me to bear –
But oh, deliver from despair!'

Strivings and wrestling seemed in vain,
Nothing I did could ease my pain;
Then gave I up my work and will,
Confessed and owned my doom was hell!

Like some poor prisoner at the bar,
Conscious of guilt, of sin and fear,
Arraigned and self-condemned I stood,
Lost in the world and in my blood!

Yet here midst blackest clouds confined,
A beam from Christ the day-star shined;
Surely, thought I, if Jesus please,
He can at once sign my release.

I, ignorant of his righteousness,
Set up my labours in its place;
Forgot for why his blood was shed,
And prayed and fasted in his stead.

He died for sinners – I am one;
Might not his blood for me atone?
Though I am nothing else but sin
Yet surely he can make me clean!

Thus light came in and I believed;
Myself forgot, and help received!
My Savior then I know I found
For, eased from guilt, no more I groaned.

Oh happy hour, in which I ceased
To mourn, for then I found a rest;
My soul and Christ were now as one –
Thy light, oh Jesus, in me shone!

Blessed be thy name, for now I know
I and my works can nothing do;
The Lord alone can ransom man:
For this the spotless lamb was slain!

When sacrifices, works, and prayer
Proved vain, and ineffectual were,
'Lo, then I come!' the Savior cried,
And bleeding, bowed his head and died.

He died for all who ever saw
No help in them, nor by the law:
I this have seen, and gladly own
Salvation is by Christ alone.

Johann Wolfgang von Goethe
1749–1832
'Wanderer's Nightsong II'
Germany
Translated by Richard Stokes

*The German writer Johann Wolfgang von Goethe believed he
would be remembered after his death not for his writing, but
for his contributions to the study of clouds. As one of the most
essential writers and thinkers in German history, he was – our
luck! – woefully incorrect.*

Wanderer's Nightsong II

Over every mountain-top
Lies peace,
In every tree-top
You scarcely feel
A breath of wind;
The little birds are hushed in the wood.
Wait, soon you too
Will be at peace.

Phillis Wheatley
c. 1753–1784
'On Virtue'
America

Kidnapped in Gambia and sold into slavery as a young girl,
Phillis Wheatley became the first African-American to publish a
book of poetry. Her work, largely devotional in content, deployed
complicated metres and earned her a great deal of international
acclaim. In a very real way, her work directly inflected and
possibly even helped catalyse British Romanticism; Samuel
Taylor Coleridge borrowed a number of concepts and bits of
language directly from Wheatley's poetry.

On Virtue

O thou bright jewel in my aim I strive
To comprehend thee. Thine own words declare
Wisdom is higher than a fool can reach.
I cease to wonder, and no more attempt
Thine height t'explore, or fathom thy profound.
But, O my soul, sink not into despair,
Virtue is near thee, and with gentle hand
Would now embrace thee, hovers o'er thine head.
Fain would the heaven-born soul with her converse,
Then seek, then court her for her promised bliss.
Auspicious queen, thine heavenly pinions spread,
And lead celestial *Chastity* along;
Lo! now her sacred retinue descends,
Arrayed in glory from the orbs above.
Attend me, *Virtue*, thro' my youthful years!
O leave me not to the false joys of time!
But guide my steps to endless life and bliss.
Greatness, or *Goodness*, say what I shall call thee,
To give an higher appellation still.
Teach me a better strain, a nobler lay,
O Thou, enthroned with Cherubs in the realms of day!

William Blake
1757–1827
'Auguries of Innocence'
England

*One of the most important British Romantics, Blake's art –
visual, theological and poetic – went largely unrecognized in his
lifetime, but his visionary work would go on to influence the entire
trajectory of Western spiritual verse.*

Auguries of Innocence

To see a World in a Grain of Sand
And a Heaven in a Wild Flower
Hold Infinity in the palm of your hand
And Eternity in an hour
A Robin Red breast in a Cage
Puts all Heaven in a Rage
A Dove house filld with Doves & Pigeons
Shudders Hell thr' all its regions
A dog starvd at his Masters Gate
Predicts the ruin of the State
A Horse misusd upon the Road
Calls to Heaven for Human blood
Each outcry of the hunted Hare
A fibre from the Brain does tear
A Skylark wounded in the wing
A Cherubim does cease to sing
The Game Cock clipd & armd for fight
Does the Rising Sun affright
Every Wolfs & Lions howl
Raises from Hell a Human Soul
The wild deer, wandring here & there
Keeps the Human Soul from Care
The Lamb misusd breeds Public Strife
And yet forgives the Butchers knife
The Bat that flits at close of Eve
Has left the Brain that wont Believe
The Owl that calls upon the Night
Speaks the Unbelievers fright
He who shall hurt the little Wren
Shall never be belovd by Men

He who the Ox to wrath has movd
Shall never be by Woman lovd
The wanton Boy that kills the Fly
Shall feel the Spiders enmity
He who torments the Chafers Sprite
Weaves a Bower in endless Night
The Catterpiller on the Leaf
Repeats to thee thy Mothers grief
Kill not the Moth nor Butterfly
For the Last Judgment draweth nigh
He who shall train the Horse to War
Shall never pass the Polar Bar
The Beggars Dog & Widows Cat
Feed them & thou wilt grow fat
The Gnat that sings his Summers Song
Poison gets from Slanders tongue
The poison of the Snake & Newt
Is the sweat of Envys Foot
The poison of the Honey Bee
Is the Artists Jealousy
The Princes Robes & Beggars Rags
Are Toadstools on the Misers Bags
A Truth I told with bad intent
Beats all the Lies you can invent
It is right it should be so
Man was made for Joy & Woe
And when this we rightly know
Thro the World we safely go
Joy & Woe are woven fine
A Clothing for the soul divine
Under every grief & pine
Runs a joy with silken twine

The Babe is more swaddling Bands
Throughout all these Human Lands
Tools were made & Born were hands
Every Farmer Understands
Every Tear from Every Eye
Becomes a Babe in Eternity
This is caught by Females bright
And returnd to its own delight
The Bleat the Bark Bellow & Roar
Are Waves that Beat on Heavens Shore
The Babe that weeps the Rod beneath
Writes Revenge in realms of Death
The Beggars Rags fluttering in Air
Does to Rags the Heavens tear
The Soldier armd with Sword & Gun
Palsied strikes the Summers Sun
The poor Mans Farthing is worth more
Than all the Gold on Africs Shore
One Mite wrung from the Labrers hands
Shall buy & sell the Misers Lands
Or if protected from on high
Does that whole Nation sell & buy
He who mocks the Infants Faith
Shall be mockd in Age & Death
He who shall teach the Child to Doubt
The rotting Grave shall neer get out
He who respects the Infants faith
Triumphs over Hell & Death
The Childs Toys & the Old Mans Reasons
Are the Fruits of the Two seasons
The Questioner who sits so sly
Shall never know how to Reply

He who replies to words of Doubt
Doth put the Light of Knowledge out
The Strongest Poison ever known
Came from Caesars Laurel Crown
Nought can Deform the Human Race
Like to the Armours iron brace
When Gold & Gems adorn the Plow
To peaceful Arts shall Envy Bow
A Riddle or the Crickets Cry
Is to Doubt a fit Reply
The Emmets Inch & Eagles Mile
Make Lame Philosophy to smile
He who Doubts from what he sees
Will neer Believe do what you Please
If the Sun & Moon should Doubt
Theyd immediately Go out
To be in a Passion you Good may Do
But no Good if a Passion is in you
The Whore & Gambler by the State
Licencd build that Nations Fate
The Harlots cry from Street to Street
Shall weave Old Englands winding Sheet
The Winners Shout the Losers Curse
Dance before dead Englands Hearse
Every Night & every Morn
Some to Misery are Born
Every Morn and every Night
Some are Born to sweet delight
Some are Born to sweet delight
Some are Born to Endless Night
We are led to Believe a Lie
When we see not Thro the Eye

Which was Born in a Night to perish in a Night
When the Soul Slept in Beams of Light
God Appears & God is Light
To those poor Souls who dwell in Night
But does a Human Form Display
To those who Dwell in Realms of day

Kobayashi Issa
1763–1828
Japan
Translated by Robert Hass

It is easy to intend to be good, much harder to actually do it. As St Augustine famously prayed, 'Da mihi castitatem et continentiam, sed noli modo' – 'Give me chastity and continence, but not yet.'

1.

All the time I pray to Buddha
I keep on
    killing mosquitoes.

2.

Even with insects –
some can sing,
    some can't.

3.

The snow is melting
and the village is flooded
    with children.

John Clare
1793–1864
'I Am!'
England

One of the great poets of rural life, John Clare struggled with
alcoholism and mental health issues. Though he spent most of his
final years in an asylum, Clare would eventually be remembered
as one of the most important British poets of the nineteenth
century.

I Am!

I am – yet what I am none cares or knows;
My friends forsake me like a memory lost:
I am the self-consumer of my woes –
They rise and vanish in oblivious host,
Like shadows in love's frenzied stifled throes
And yet I am, and live – like vapours tossed

Into the nothingness of scorn and noise,
Into the living sea of waking dreams,
Where there is neither sense of life or joys,
But the vast shipwreck of my life's esteems;
Even the dearest that I loved the best
Are strange – nay, rather, stranger than the rest.

I long for scenes where man hath never trod
A place where woman never smiled or wept
There to abide with my Creator, God,
And sleep as I in childhood sweetly slept,
Untroubling and untroubled where I lie
The grass below – above the vaulted sky.

John Keats
1795–1821
'Ode on a Grecian Urn'
England

For John Keats nearly everything was divine, from his beloved
Fanny Brawne to a nightingale to melancholy itself. But 'Ode on a
Grecian Urn' contains perhaps his best divine articulation; or, if
not best, then at least most bald: 'Beauty is truth, truth beauty, –
that is all / Ye know on earth, and all ye need to know.'

Ode on a Grecian Urn

Thou still unravish'd bride of quietness,
    Thou foster-child of silence and slow time,
Sylvan historian, who canst thus express
    A flowery tale more sweetly than our rhyme:
What leaf-fring'd legend haunts about thy shape
      Of deities or mortals, or of both,
          In Tempe or the dales of Arcady?
      What men or gods are these? What maidens loth?
What mad pursuit? What struggle to escape?
      What pipes and timbrels? What wild ecstasy?

Heard melodies are sweet, but those unheard
    Are sweeter; therefore, ye soft pipes, play on;
Not to the sensual ear, but, more endear'd,
    Pipe to the spirit ditties of no tone:
Fair youth, beneath the trees, thou canst not leave
      Thy song, nor ever can those trees be bare;
          Bold Lover, never, never canst thou kiss,
Though winning near the goal yet, do not grieve;
      She cannot fade, though thou hast not thy bliss,
          For ever wilt thou love, and she be fair!

Ah, happy, happy boughs! that cannot shed
    Your leaves, nor ever bid the Spring adieu;
And, happy melodist, unwearied,
    For ever piping songs for ever new;
More happy love! more happy, happy love!
      For ever warm and still to be enjoy'd,
          For ever panting, and for ever young;

All breathing human passion far above,
    That leaves a heart high-sorrowful and cloy'd,
        A burning forehead, and a parching tongue.

Who are these coming to the sacrifice?
    To what green altar, O mysterious priest,
Lead'st thou that heifer lowing at the skies,
    And all her silken flanks with garlands drest?
What little town by river or sea shore,
    Or mountain-built with peaceful citadel,
        Is emptied of this folk, this pious morn?
And, little town, thy streets for evermore
    Will silent be; and not a soul to tell
        Why thou art desolate, can e'er return.

O Attic shape! Fair attitude! with brede
    Of marble men and maidens overwrought,
With forest branches and the trodden weed;
    Thou, silent form, dost tease us out of thought
As doth eternity: Cold Pastoral!
    When old age shall this generation waste,
        Thou shalt remain, in midst of other woe
Than ours, a friend to man, to whom thou say'st,
    'Beauty is truth, truth beauty – that is all
        Ye know on earth, and all ye need to know.'

Mirza Ghalib
1797–1869
'For the Raindrop'
India
Translated by Jane Hirshfield

One of the last great poets of the Mughal Empire, Mirza Ghalib
wrote in both Urdu and Persian. In this piece, he suggests,
'Unbearable pain becomes its own cure'. Ghalib, like many
spiritual poets, believed that suffering might thin the partition
between humans and the divine.

For the Raindrop

For the raindrop, joy is in entering the river –
Unbearable pain becomes its own cure.
Travel far enough into sorrow, tears turn into sighing; in this way
      we learn how water can die into air.
When, after heavy rain, the storm clouds disperse, is it not that
      they've wept themselves clear to the end?
If you want to know the miracle, how wind can polish a mirror,
Look: the shining glass grows green in spring.
It's the roses unfolding, Ghalib, that creates the desire to see –
In every color and circumstance,
May the eyes be open for what comes.

Elizabeth Barrett Browning
1806–1861
'Grief'
England

One of Emily Dickinson's favourite poets, Browning nearly succeeded William Wordsworth in the Poet Laureateship, a role that would have been almost unimaginable for a woman to hold. In fact, perhaps it was unimaginable – they gave the job to Alfred Tennyson.

Grief

I tell you, hopeless grief is passionless;
That only men incredulous of despair,
Half-taught in anguish, through the midnight air
Beat upward to God's throne in loud access
Of shrieking and reproach. Full desertness,
In souls as countries, lieth silent-bare
Under the blanching, vertical eye-glare
Of the absolute heavens. Deep-hearted man, express
Grief for thy dead in silence like to death –
Most like a monumental statue set
In everlasting watch and moveless woe
Till itself crumble to the dust beneath.
Touch it; the marble eyelids are not wet:
If it could weep, it could arise and go.

Frederick Douglass
1818–1895
'A Parody'
America

*Some spiritual poetry is written tongue firmly in cheek. Here,
Frederick Douglass writes a scorching parody poem condemning
the hypocrisy of the Southern Church during the Antebellum
South.*

A Parody

Come, saints and sinners, hear me tell
How pious priests whip Jack and Nell,
And women buy and children sell,
And preach all sinners down to hell,
    And sing of heavenly union.

They'll bleat and baa, dona' like goats,
Gorge down black sheep, and strain at motes,
Array their backs in fine black coats,
Then seize their negroes by their throats
    And choke for heavenly union.

They'll church you if you sip a dram,
And damn you if you steal a lamb,
Yet rob old Tony, Doll, and Sam
Of human rights and bread and ham –
    Kidnapper's heavenly union.

They'll loudly talk of Christ's reward
And bind his image with a cord,
And scold and swing the lash abhorred,
And sell their brother in the Lord
    To handcuffed heavenly union.

They'll read and sing a sacred song,
And make a prayer both loud and long,
And teach the right and do the wrong,
Hailing the brother, sister throng
    With words of heavenly union.

We wonder how such saints can sing
Or praise the Lord upon the wing,
Who roar and scold, and whip and sting,
And to their slaves and mammon cling
    In guilty conscience union.

They'll raise tobacco, corn, and rye,
And drive and thieve, and cheat and lie,
And lay up treasures in the sky
By making switch and cowskin fly,
    In hope of heavenly union.

They'll crack old Tony on the skull,
And preach and roar like Bashan bull,
Or braying ass, of mischief full,
Then seize old Jacob by the wool,
    And pull for heavenly union.

A roaring, ranting, sleek man-thief
Who lived on mutton, veal, and beef,
Yet never would afford relief
To needy, sable sons of grief
    Was big with heavenly union.

'Love not the world,' the preacher said,
And winked his eye, and shook his head;
He seized on Tom, and Dick, and Ned,
Cut short their meat and clothes and bread,
    Yet still loved heavenly union.

Another preacher whining spoke
Of One whose heart for sinners broke:
He tied old Nanny to an oak
And drew the blood at every stroke,
    And prayed for heavenly union.

Two others oped their iron jaws,
And waved their children-stealing paws;
There sat their children in gewgaws;
By stinting negroes' backs and maws,
    They kept up heavenly union.

All good from Jack another takes,
And entertains their flirts and rakes,
Who dress as sleek as glossy snakes,
And cram their mouths with sweetened cakes;
    And this goes down for union.

Emily Dickinson
1830–1886
'I prayed, at first, a little Girl'
America

*Emily Dickinson once ended a letter to her young cousins by
saying, 'Let Emily sing for you because she cannot pray.' I imagine
this poem as the song she might have sung then, in lieu of a prayer.*

I prayed at first, a little Girl

I prayed, at first, a little Girl,
Because they told me to –
But stopped, when qualified to guess
How prayer would feel – to me –

If I believed God looked around,
Each time my Childish eye
Fixed full, and steady, on his own
In Childish honesty –

And told him what I'd like, today,
And parts of his far plan
That baffled me –
The mingled side
Of his Divinity –

And often since, in Danger,
I count the force 'twould be
To have a God so strong as that
To hold my life for me

Till I could take the Balance
That tips so frequent, now,
It takes me all the while to poise –
And then – it doesn't stay –

Uvavnuk
Nineteenth century
'The Great Sea'
Igloolik, northern Canada
Translated by Jane Hirshfield

The great Inuit poet and spiritual healer Uvavnuk was said to
have been struck by a meteor that bestowed her with visionary
powers. The movement of the divines celebrated in this
poem – the sea and the wind – feel in her language like ecstatic
occasions for great celebration.

The Great Sea

The great sea
frees me, moves me,
as a strong river carries a weed.
Earth and her strong winds
move me, take me away,
and my soul is swept up in joy.

Gerard Manley Hopkins
1844–1889
'God's Grandeur'
England

The Jesuit priest Gerard Manley Hopkins's poems weren't really celebrated until the middle of the twentieth century. Part of this inattention is likely because his poems were so radically different from anything else being written – their bombastic, concussive language sounds startling even today. When you read a poem like 'God's Grandeur' out loud, you can hear Hopkins's fervent faith. Maybe you can even taste it.

God's Grandeur

The world is charged with the grandeur of God.
      It will flame out, like shining from shook foil;
      It gathers to a greatness, like the ooze of oil
Crushed. Why do men then now not reck his rod?
Generations have trod, have trod, have trod;
      And all is seared with trade; bleared, smeared with toil;
      And wears man's smudge and shares man's smell: the soil
Is bare now, nor can foot feel, being shod.

And for all this, nature is never spent;
      There lives the dearest freshness deep down things;
And though the last lights off the black West went
      Oh, morning, at the brown brink eastward, springs –
Because the Holy Ghost over the bent
      World broods with warm breast and with ah! bright wings.

Rabindranath Tagore
1861–1941
'The Temple of Gold'
India

Here is Rabindranath Tagore's incisive poem against the excesses
of the wealthy, especially when those excesses were carried out in
the name of faith.

The Temple of Gold

'Sire,' announced the servant to the King, 'the saint Narottam never deigns to step into your royal temple. He is singing God's praise under the trees by the open road. The temple is empty of all worshippers. They flock round him like bees round the fragrant white lotus, leaving the golden jar of honey unheeded.'

The King, vexed at heart, went to the spot where Narottam sat on the grass. He asked him, 'Father, why leave my temple of the golden dome, and sit on the dust outside to preach God's love?'

'Because God is not there in your temple,' said Narottam.

The King frowned and said, 'Do you know twenty millions of gold have been spent on that marvel of art, and the temple was duly consecrated to God with costly rites?'

'Yes, I know,' answered Narottam. 'It was the dread year when thousands of your people lost their homes in fire and stood at your door for help in vain. And God said, "The poor creature who can give no shelter to his brothers would aspire to build my house!" Thus he took his place with the shelterless under the trees by the road. And that golden bubble is empty of all but hot vapor of pride.'

The King cried in anger, 'Leave my land!'

Calmly said the saint, 'Yes, banish me where you have banished my God.'

Constantine Cavafy
1863–1933
'Body, Remember'
Egypt/Greece
Translated by Edmund Keeley and Philip Sherrard

*The body can be its own divine. So can memory. In this poem by
the Greek titan Constantine Cavafy we see the body and memory
each trying to reconcile the other's divinity.*

Body, Remember

Body, remember not only how much you were loved,
not only the beds you lay on,
but also those desires that glowed openly
in eyes that looked at you,
trembled for you in the voices –
only some chance obstacle frustrated them.
Now that it's all finally in the past,
it seems almost as if you gave yourself
to those desires too – how they glowed,
remember, in eyes that looked at you,
remember, body, how they trembled for you in those voices.

W. B. Yeats
1865–1939
'The Second Coming'
Ireland

*One of the most famous poems in the English language and also
one of the darkest – it seems as if most of human history has been
a study in various 'rough beasts' slouching their way into power.*

The Second Coming

Turning and turning in the widening gyre
The falcon cannot hear the falconer;
Things fall apart; the centre cannot hold;
Mere anarchy is loosed upon the world,
The blood-dimmed tide is loosed, and everywhere
The ceremony of innocence is drowned;
The best lack all conviction, while the worst
Are full of passionate intensity.

Surely some revelation is at hand;
Surely the Second Coming is at hand.
The Second Coming! Hardly are those words out
When a vast image out of Spiritus Mundi
Troubles my sight: a waste of desert sand;
A shape with lion body and the head of a man,
A gaze blank and pitiless as the sun,
Is moving its slow thighs, while all about it
Wind shadows of the indignant desert birds.

The darkness drops again but now I know
That twenty centuries of stony sleep
Were vexed to nightmare by a rocking cradle,
And what rough beast, its hour come round at last,
Slouches towards Bethlehem to be born?

Rainer Maria Rilke
1875–1926
'The Second Duino Elegy'
Austria
Translated by David Young

The German-language poet Rainer Maria Rilke is best known for his instructive Letters to a Young Poet. *His own verse, however, takes on some of the most difficult and esoteric spiritual goals. In this poem he works to invoke all he knows to be terrible and frightening – an angel, a god, a word.*

The Second Duino Elegy

Every angel is terrible.
        And still, alas
                knowing all that
I serenade you
        you almost deadly
                birds of the soul.
Where are the days of Tobias
        when one of these
                brightest of creatures
stood
        at the simple front door
                disguised a little
for the trip
        and not so frightening
                (a young man
like the one
        who looked curiously
                out at him).
If the dangerous archangel
        took one step now
                down toward us
from behind the stars
        our heartbeats
                rising like thunder
would kill us.
                Who are you?
Creation's spoiled darlings
        among the first to be perfect
                a chain of mountains

peaks and ridges
                red in the morning light
                            of all creation
the blossoming godhead's pollen
                joints of pure light
                            corridors
staircases
                thrones
                            pockets of essence
ecstasy shields
                tumultuous storms
                            of delightful feelings
then suddenly
                separate
                mirrors
gathering the beauty
                that streamed away from them
                            back to their own faces again.

For as we feel
                we evaporate
                            oh we
breathe ourselves out
                and away
                            emberglow to emberglow
we give off a fainter smell.
                It's true that someone
                            may say to us
'You're in my blood
                this room
                            the spring
is filling with you' . . .
                What good is that?
                            he can't keep us

we vanish inside him
            around him.
                        And the beautiful
oh who can hold them back?
            It's endless:
                        appearance shines
from their faces
            disappearing – like dew
                        rising from morning grass
we breathe away
            what is ours
                        like steam from a hot dish.
Oh smile where are you going?
            Oh lifted glance
                        new, warm
receding wave of the heart
            woe is me?
                        it's *all* of us.
Does the outer space
            into which we dissolve
                        taste of us at all?
Do the angels absorb
            only what's theirs
                        what streamed away from them
or do they sometimes get
            as if by mistake
                        a little of our being too?
Are we mixed into
            their features
                        as slightly
as that vague look
            in the faces
                        of pregnant women?

In their swirling
        return to themselves
                they don't notice it.
(How could they notice it?)

Lovers, if they knew how
        might say strange things
                in the night air.
For it seems
        that all things try
                to conceal us.
See, the trees *are*
        and the houses we live in
                still hold their own,
It's just we
        who pass everything by
                like air being traded
for air.
        And all things agree
                to keep quiet about us
maybe half to shame us
        and half from a hope
                they can't express.

Lovers, you who are
        each other's satisfaction
                I ask you about us.
You hold each other.
        Does that settle it?
                You see
it sometimes happens
        that my hands
                grow conscious

of each other
        or that my used face
                shelters itself
within them.
        That gives me
                a slight sensation.
But who'd claim from that
        to *exist*?
                You though
who grow
        by each other's ecstasy
                until drowning
you beg 'no *more!*'
        you who under
                each other's hands
become more abundant
        like the grapes
                of great vintages
fading at times
        but only because
                the other completely
takes over –
        I ask you about us.
                I know
that touch
        is a blessing for you
                because the caress lasts
because what you cover
        so tenderly
                does not disappear
because you can sense
        underneath the touch
                some kind of pure

duration.
       Somehow eternity
            almost seems possible
as you embrace.
       And yet
            when you've got past
the fear in that first
       exchange of glances
            the mooning at the window
and that first walk
       together in the garden
            one time:
lovers, *are* you the same?
       When you lift
            each other to your lips
mouth to mouth
       drink to drink –
            oh how oddly
the drinker seems
       to withdraw
            from the act of drinking.

Weren't you astonished
       by the discretion
            of human gesture
on Attic grave steles?
       Didn't love and parting
            sit so lightly
on shoulders
       that they seemed
            to be made of a substance

different from ours?
           Do you recall
                      how the hands rest
without any pressure
           though there is great
                      strength in the torsos?
Those figures spoke
           a language of self-mastery:
                      we've come to this point
this is us
           touching this way
                      the gods
may push us around
           but that is something
                      for them to decide.
If only we too
           could discover an orchard
                      some pure, contained
human, narrow
           strip of land
                      between river and rock.
For our own heart
           outgrows us
                      just as it did them
and we can't follow it
           by gazing at pictures
                      that soothe it
or at godlike bodies
           that restrain it
                      by their very size.

Muhammad Iqbal
1877–1938
Pakistan
Translated by Mustansir Dalvi

*Muhammad Iqbal was not only one of the great poets of the
Muslim world but also one of its great political leaders. In this
poem, he writes about the irrepressibility of faith – more resilient
than death, yes, but also more resilient than political suppression.*

These are the days of lightning,
every haystack set aflame –
nothing, desert or garden,
is free from its bloom.

The old ways are only fuel
to this new fire, even
the Prophet's all-embracing cloak
could be consumed.

Yet, if today
Abraham's faith were to be reborn,
this very fire
could nourish a new garden.

Yosano Akiko
1878–1942
Japan
Translated by Sandford Goldstein and Seishi Shinodo

Throughout history patriarchal cultures have sought to deprive women of basic rights and liberties, and throughout history women have used whatever resources were at their disposal – their wits, their beauty – to get back at them. In this poem, Yosano Akiko celebrates her own beauty as an almost divine instrument of wrath.

To punish
Men for their endless sins,
God gave me
This fair skin,
This long black hair!

Sarojini Naidu
1879–1949
'In the Bazaars of Hyderabad'
India

Sarojini Naidu, nicknamed 'the nightingale of India', was an
important Indian civil rights leader and activist. In many of her
poems we see her land and her people becoming divines unto
themselves.

In the Bazaars of Hyderabad

What do you sell O ye merchants?
Richly your wares are displayed.
Turbans of crimson and silver,
Tunics of purple brocade,
Mirrors with panels of amber,
Daggers with handles of jade.

What do you weigh, O ye vendors?
Saffron and lentil and rice.
What do you grind, O ye maidens?
Sandalwood, henna, and spice.
What do you call, O ye pedlars?
Chessmen and ivory dice.

What do you make, O ye goldsmiths?
Wristlet and anklet and ring,
Bells for the feet of blue pigeons
Frail as a dragon-fly's wing,
Girdles of gold for dancers,
Scabbards of gold for the king.

What do you cry, O ye fruitmen?
Citron, pomegranate, and plum.
What do you play, O musicians?
Cithar, sarangi and drum.
What do you chant, O magicians?
Spells for aeons to come.

What do you weave, O ye flower-girls
With tassels of azure and red?
Crowns for the brow of a bridegroom,
Chaplets to garland his bed.
Sheets of white blossoms new-garnered
To perfume the sleep of the dead.

Delmira Agustini
1886–1914
'Inextinguishables'
Uruguay
Translated by Eloisa Amezcua

*Agustini describes a beloved as looking 'Miraculous when alive,
miraculous when dead'. This poet, who was tragically murdered
by her ex-husband at the age of twenty-seven, left us with a body
of incandescent verse that feels truly miraculous.*

Inextinguishables

Oh, you who sleep so deep you do not wake!
Miraculous when alive, miraculous when dead,
And in death and life eternally open,

Some night in grief I find your eyes

Under a cloth's shadow or the moon's lace.
I drink from them the Calm as in a lake.
For profound, for quiet, for good, for serene

Each one looks like a bed or a grave.

Gabriela Mistral
1889–1957
'The Return'
Chile
Translated by Ursula K. Le Guin

The 'Master' in Gabriela Mistral's poem is like the 'Master' in Emily Dickinson's 'Master Letters', which Dickinson wrote, but never sent, to a mysterious 'Master'. We meet the 'Master' of Mistral's poem as we are naked and 'Soiled, like sheep'. And, like Dickinson, Mistral keeps us firmly rooted on the side of mystery.

The Return

Naked we return to our Master,
Soiled, like sheep
from muddy roads and thickets,
and naked return to the high place
whose light shows us naked.
And the Homeland we come to
stares at us, unrecognizing.

But we never were released
from the choir of the Thrones
and Dominations,
and never had any names,
since all names name the One.

We dream mothers, brothers,
and the wheel of day and night,
and never depart from
that day without escape.
We thought we sang, and rested,
and then rejoined the song,
but there was never anything
but the unceasing hymn.

And we were never soldiers,
or masters or prentices,
since we knew dimly,
that we only played at Time,
being children of Eternity.
And we never left that Homeland,
and the rest has all been dreams,
games of children in a vast courtyard:
festivals, wars, loves, griefs.

Sleeping, we made journeys
and arrived at no place,
and wearied our guardian Angels
with our comings and goings.

And the Angels laughed
at our sorrows and delights,
our searches and discoveries,
our pitiful gains and losses.

We fell down and got up.
faces crumpled with weeping,
and all we laughed or cried at,
all our roads and byways,
leavetakings and arrivals –
all we did they did with us,
always right beside us.

And the laborious tasks,
never, never did we learn them:
song, when there was singing,
came broken from the throat.

Day after day
playing at gardening, dancing, singing,
at work without a Master,
at travel without a road,
and at names without things,
and at leaving without arriving,
we were children, children,
inconstant, babbling.

And we come back, futile,
so tired, and emptyhanded,
stammering names of 'homelands'
that we never reached.

Anna Akhmatova
1889–1966
From 'Requiem'
Russia
Translated by Judith Hemschemeyer

In 'Requiem', one of the great poems of the twentieth century,
Akhmatova masterfully braids her grief over her son's unjust
imprisonment and the miserable fate of her country with
iconography from the Christian faith.

INSTEAD OF A PREFACE

In the terrible years of the Yezhov terror, I spent seventeen months in the prison lines of Leningrad. Once, someone 'recognized' me. Then a woman with bluish lips standing behind me, who, of course, had never heard me called by name before, woke up from the stupor to which everyone had succumbed and whispered in my ear (everyone spoke in whispers there):

'Can you describe this?'

And I answered: 'Yes, I can.'

Then something that looked like a smile passed over what had once been her face.

April 1, 1957
Leningrad

IX

Now madness half shadows
My soul with its wing,
And makes it drunk with fiery wine
And beckons toward the black ravine.

And I've finally realized
That I must give in,
Overhearing myself
Raving as if it were somebody else.

And it does not allow me to take
Anything of mine with me

(No matter how I plead with it,
No matter how I supplicate):

Not the terrible eyes of my son –
Suffering turned to stone,
Not the day of the terror,
Not the hour I met with him in prison,

Not the sweet coolness of his hands,
Not the trembling shadow of the lindens,
Not the far-off, fragile sound –
Of the final words of consolation.

May 4, 1940
Fountain House

X

CRUCIFIXION

'Do not weep for Me, Mother, I am in the grave.'

1

A choir of angels sang the praises of that momentous hour,
And the heavens dissolved in fire.
To his Father He said: 'Why hast Thou forsaken me!'
And to his Mother: 'Oh, do not weep for Me . . .'

1940
Fountain House

2

Mary Magdalene beat her breast and sobbed,
The beloved disciple turned to stone,
But where the silent Mother stood, there
No one glanced and no one would have dared.

1943
Tashkent

EPILOGUE I

I learned how faces fall,
How terror darts from under eyelids,
How suffering traces lines
Of stiff cuneiform on cheeks,
How locks of ashen-blonde or black
Turn silver suddenly,
Smiles fade on submissive lips
And fear trembles in a dry laugh.
And I pray not for myself alone,
But for all those who stood there with me
In cruel cold, and in July's heat,
At that blind, red wall.

EPILOGUE II

Once more the day of remembrance draws near.
I see, I hear, I feel you:

The one they almost had to drag at the end,
And the one who tramps her native land no more,

And the one who, tossing her beautiful head,
Said: 'Coming here's like coming home.'

I'd like to name them all by name,
But the list has been confiscated and is nowhere to be found.

I have woven a wide mantle for them
From their meager, overheard words.

I will remember them always and everywhere,
I will never forget them no matter what comes.

And if they gag my exhausted mouth
Through which a hundred million scream,

Then may the people remember me
On the eve of my remembrance day.

And if ever in this country
They decide to erect a monument to me,

I consent to that honor
Under these conditions – that it stand

Neither by the sea, where I was born:
My last tie with the sea is broken,

Nor in the tsar's garden near the cherished pine stump,
Where an inconsolable shade looks for me,

But here, where I stood for three hundred hours,
And where they never unbolted the doors for me.

This, lest in blissful death
I forget the rumbling of the Black Marias,

Forget how that detested door slammed shut
And an old woman howled like a wounded animal.

And may the melting snow stream like tears
From my motionless lids of bronze,

And a prison dove coo in the distance,
And the ships of the Neva sail calmly on.

March 1940

Osip Mandelstam
1891–1938
Russia
Translated by Clarence Brown and W. S. Merwin

Some prayers are foxhole prayers, desperate and hopeless. This tiny poem by the radical Osip Mandelstam feels like a foxhole prayer to me. Endlessly hounded by the Stalinist government, Mandelstam eventually died in a labour camp, but not before penning some of the century's most affecting verse.

O Lord, help me to live through this night –
I'm in terror for life, your slave:
to live in Petersburg is to sleep in a grave.

Edith Södergran
1892–1923
'A Life'
Sweden
Translated by Averill Curdy

Where does one look for the divine? The stars, a wave, under a stone? Hafez said, 'Start seeing God everywhere, but keep it secret.'

A Life

That the stars are adamant
everyone understands –
but I won't give up seeking joy on each blue wave
or peace below every grey stone.
If happiness never comes, what is a life?
A lily withers in the sand
and if its nature has failed? The tide
                                    washes the beach at night.
What is the fly looking for on the spider's web?
What does a dayfly make of its hours?
(Two wings creased over a hollow body.)

Black will never turn to white –
yet the perfume of our struggle lingers
as each morning fresh flowers
spring up from hell.

The day will come
when the earth is emptied, the skies collapse
and all goes still –
when nothing remains but the dayfly
                                    folded in a leaf.
But no one knows it.

Marina Tsvetaeva
1892–1941
From *Poems to Czechia*
Russia
Translated by Jean Valentine and Ilya Kaminsky

*Tsvetaeva, who lived through the Russian Revolution and the
unimaginable famine and hardship that followed, celebrates here
the human capacity to refuse life in a broken world; 'time / to
give back to God his ticket', she writes, and it almost sounds like a
suggestion.*

A black mountain
has blocked out the light of the Earth.
Time – time – time
to give back to God his ticket.

I refuse to – be. In
the madhouse of the inhumans
I refuse to – live. To swim
with the current of human spines.

I have no need for holes
in my ears, no need for seeing eyes.
To your mad world
one answer – to refuse.

María Sabina
1894–1985
From 'The Midnight Velada'
Mexico
Translated by Eloisa de Estrada Gonzales and Henry Munn

*María Sabina was a Mazatec Mexican shaman and oral poet.
Her vivid, mystical chants came to her during sacred mushroom
ceremonies (veladas). This is one such chant, preserved for us by
her contemporary, fellow Mazatec Álvaro Estrada.*

The Midnight Velada

I am the woman of the great expanse of the water
I am the woman of the expanse of the divine sea
I am a river woman
the woman of the flowing water
a woman who examines and searches
a woman with hands and measure
a woman mistress of measure

I am a saint woman
a spirit woman
I am a woman of clarity
a woman of the day
a clean woman
a ready woman
because I am a woman who lightnings
a woman who thunders
a woman who shouts
a woman who whistles

Morning Star woman
Southern Cross woman
Constellation of the Sandal woman, says
Hook Constellation woman, says
that is your clock, says
that is your book, says
I am the little woman of the ancient fountain, says
I am the little woman of the sacred fountain, says

hummingbird woman, says
woman who has sprouted wings, says

thus do I descend primordial
thus do I descend significant
I descend with tenderness
I descend with the dew
your book, my Father, says
your book, my Father, says
clown woman beneath the water, says
clown woman beneath the sea, says
because I am the child of Christ
the child of Mary, says

I am a woman of letters, says
I am a book woman, says
nobody can close my book, says
nobody can take my book away from me, says
my book encountered beneath the water, says
my book of prayers

I am a woman and a mother, says
a mother woman beneath the water, says
a woman of good words, says
a woman of music, says
a wise diviner woman

I am a lagoon woman, says
I am a ladder woman, says
I am the Morning Star woman, says
I am a woman comet, says
I am the woman who goes through the water, says
I am the woman who goes through the sea, says

Xu Zhimo
1897–1931
'Second Farewell to Cambridge'
China
Translated by Michelle Yeh

A place can be a divine, but so can a journey. For the early modern Chinese poet Xu Zhimo, who brought innovation to Chinese poetry by using everyday colloquial language in his poems, it seems as if both the voyage and the destination inspired devotion.

Second Farewell to Cambridge

Softly I am leaving,
　　just as softly I came;
I wave softly and bid farewell
　　to the rosy clouds in the western sky.

The golden willow on the riverbank
　　is a bride in the setting sun;
Her fair reflection in the shimmering ripples
　　lingers in my heart.

The floating hearts in the soft mud
　　are beckoning to me;
In the gentle waves of Cam
　　how I'd rather be a reed!

The pool in the elm shade
　　is not a clear spring but a rainbow;
Ruffled amidst the swaying duckweeds
　　it sinks into a rainbow-like dream.

In search of a dream? With a long pole,
　　sail upstream to where the grass is greener;
In a skiff filled with starlight,
　　sing freely under the splendid stars.

But I cannot sing freely;
　　silence is the tune of farewell.
Even summer insects are quiet for me;
　　silent is Cambridge tonight.

Quietly I am leaving,
    just as quietly I came.
I raise my sleeve and wave,
    without taking away a wisp of cloud.

Federico García Lorca
1898–1936
'Farewell'
Spain

Few poets have made the border between life and death seem
thinner, more permeable, than Lorca. He once wrote: 'In every
other country death is an ending. It appears and they close the
curtains. Not in Spain. In Spain they open them.'

Farewell

If I die
leave the balcony open.

The little boy eating oranges
(I can see him from my balcony).

The reaper reaping the wheat
(I can hear him from my balcony).

If I die
leave the balcony open!

Nâzim Hikmet
1902–1963
'Things I Didn't Know I Loved'
Turkey
Translated by Randy Blasing and Mutlu Konu

Nâzim Hikmet wrote most of his work while in jail or exile. One of the myriad cruelties incarceration levies upon the prisoner is that, as the distance between them and their old life increases, so does their ability to perceive all the tiny divines that made up their old life.

Things I Didn't Know I Loved

it's 1962 March 28th
I'm sitting by the window on the Prague-Berlin train
night is falling
I never knew I liked
night descending like a tired bird on a smoky wet plain
I don't like
comparing nightfall to a tired bird

I didn't know I loved the earth
can someone who hasn't worked the earth love it
I've never worked the earth
it must be my only Platonic love

and here I've loved rivers all this time
whether motionless like this they curl skirting the hills
European hills crowned with chateaus
or whether stretched out flat as far as the eye can see
I know you can't wash in the same river even once
I know the river will bring new lights you'll never see
I know we live slightly longer than a horse but not nearly as long
          as a crow
I know this has troubled people before
                    and will trouble those after me
I know all this has been said a thousand times before
                    and will be said after me

I didn't know I loved the sky
cloudy or clear
the blue vault Andrei studied on his back at Borodino
in prison I translated both volumes of *War and Peace* into Turkish
I hear voices

not from the blue vault but from the yard
the guards are beating someone again
I didn't know I loved trees
bare beeches near Moscow in Peredelkino
they come upon me in winter noble and modest
beeches are Russian the way poplars are Turkish
'the poplars of Izmir
losing their leaves . . .
they call me The Knife . . .
                              lover like a young tree . . .
I blow stalely mansions sky-high'
in the Ilgaz woods in 1920 I tied an embroidered linen handkerchief
                              to a pine bough for luck

I never knew I loved roads
even the asphalt kind
Vera's behind the wheel we're driving from Moscow to the Crimea
                              Koktebele
                    formerly 'Goktepé ili' in Turkish
the two of us inside a closed box
the world flows past on both sides distant and mute
I was never so close to anyone in my life
bandits stopped me on the red road between Bolu and Geredé
                              when I was eighteen
apart from my life I didn't have anything in the wagon they could take
and at eighteen our lives are what we value least
I've written this somewhere before
wading through a dark muddy street I'm going to the shadow play
Ramazan night
a paper lantern leading the way
maybe nothing like this ever happened
maybe I read it somewhere an eight-year-old boy
                              going to the shadow play

Ramazan night in Istanbul holding his grandfather's hand
   his grandfather has on a fez and is wearing the fur coat
     with a sable collar over his robe
   and there's a lantern in the servant's hand
   and I can't contain myself for joy

flowers come to mind for some reason
poppies cactuses jonquils
in the jonquil garden in Kadikoy Istanbul I kissed Marika
fresh almonds on her breath
I was seventeen
my heart on a swing touched the sky
I didn't know I loved flowers
friends sent me three red carnations in prison

I just remembered the stars
I love them too
whether I'm floored watching them from below
or whether I'm flying at their side

I have some questions for the cosmonauts
were the stars much bigger
did they look like huge jewels on black velvet
                     or apricots on orange
did you feel proud to get closer to the stars
I saw color photos of the cosmos in *Ogonek* magazine now don't
     be upset comrades but nonfigurative shall we say or abstract
     well some of them looked just like such paintings which is to
     say they were terribly figurative and concrete
my heart was in my mouth looking at them
they are our endless desire to grasp things
seeing them I could even think of death and not feel at all sad
I never knew I loved the cosmos

snow flashes in front of my eyes
both heavy wet steady snow and the dry whirling kind
I didn't know I liked snow

I never knew I loved the sun
even when setting cherry-red as now
in Istanbul too it sometimes sets in postcard colors
but you aren't about to paint it that way
I didn't know I loved the sea
                              except the Sea of Azov
or how much

I didn't know I loved clouds
whether I'm under or up above them
whether they look like giants or shaggy white beasts

moonlight the falsest the most languid the most petit-bourgeois
strikes me
I like it

I didn't know I liked rain
whether it falls like a fine net or splatters against the glass my
        heart leaves me tangled up in a net or trapped inside a drop
        and takes off for uncharted countries I didn't know I loved
        rain but why did I suddenly discover all these passions sitting
        by the window on the Prague-Berlin train
is it because I lit my sixth cigarette
one alone could kill me
is it because I'm half dead from thinking about someone back in
        Moscow
her hair straw-blond eyelashes blue

the train plunges on through the pitch-black night
I never knew I liked the night pitch-black
sparks fly from the engine
I didn't know I loved sparks
I didn't know I loved so many things and I had to wait until sixty
   to find it out sitting by the window on the Prague-Berlin train
   watching the world disappear as if on a journey of no return

Léopold Sédar Senghor
1906–2001
'Totem'
Senegal
Translated by Melvin Dixon

Senghor was, with Aimé Césaire and Léon Damas, one of the founding minds behind 'Négritude', a vein of theory promoting Black consciousness and anti-colonialist thinking across Africa and the African diaspora. In this short poem, Senghor – who would go on to become the first president of Senegal – calls the African and African diasporic community against the tyranny of European colonialism. An idea, a movement, a people – each of these is a powerful divine.

Totem

I must hide him down in my deepest veins
The Ancestor whose stormy skin
Streaks with lightning and thunder
He is the guardian animal I must hide
Lest I burst the dam of scandal.
He is my loyal blood demanding loyalty,
Protecting my naked pride against myself
And the arrogance of fortunate races . . .

Faiz Ahmed Faiz
1911–1984
'Before You Came'
Pakistan
Translated by Naomi Lazard

Some romance gets so close to the divine it practically glows.
Or, as in this poem by the Pakistani maestro Faiz Ahmed Faiz,
it might turn the sky back into the sky.

Before You Came

Before you came,
things were as they should be:
the sky was the dead-end of sight,
the road was just a road, wine merely wine.

Now everything is like my heart,
a color at the edge of blood:
the grey of your absence, the color of poison, of thorns,
the gold when we meet, the season ablaze,
the yellow of autumn, the red of flowers, of flames,
and the black when you cover the earth
with the coal of dead fires.

And the sky, the road, the glass of wine?
The sky is a shirt wet with tears,
the road a vein about to break,
and the glass of wine a mirror in which
the sky, the road, the world keep changing.

Don't leave now that you're here —
Stay. So the world may become like itself again: so the sky may be
        the sky,
the road a road,
and the glass of wine not a mirror, just a glass of wine.

Czesław Miłosz
1911–2004
'Dedication'
Poland
Translated by Czesław Miłosz

*There are constant debates in the literary world about 'the
purpose of poetry', endless conversations about what poems can
and can't do. In this poem, Milosz says it as well as it has ever
been said: 'What is poetry which does not save / Nations or
people?'*

Dedication

You whom I could not save
Listen to me.
Try to understand this simple speech as I would be ashamed of
      another.
I swear, there is in me no wizardry of words.
I speak to you with silence like a cloud or a tree.

What strengthened me, for you was lethal.
You mixed up farewell to an epoch with the beginning of a new one,
Inspiration of hatred with lyrical beauty;
Blind force with accomplished shape.

Here is a valley of shallow Polish rivers. And an immense bridge
Going into white fog. Here is a broken city;
And the wind throws the screams of gulls on your grave
When I am talking with you.

What is poetry which does not save
Nations or people?
A connivance with official lies,
A song of drunkards whose throats will be cut in a moment,
Readings for sophomore girls.
That I wanted good poetry without knowing it,
That I discovered, late, its salutary aim,
In this and only this I find salvation.

They used to pour millet on graves or poppy seeds
To feed the dead who would come disguised as birds.
I put this book here for you, who once lived
So that you should visit us no more.

Edmond Jabès
1912–1991
'At the Threshold of the Book'
France/Egypt
Translated by Rosmarie Waldrop

One of the great Jewish mystical poets of the twentieth century, Jabès once wrote: 'For me the words "Jew" and "God" are, it is true, metaphors. "God" is the metaphor for emptiness; "Jew" stands for the torment of God, of emptiness.'

At the Threshold of the Book

*Mark the first page of the book with a red marker. For,
in the beginning, the wound is invisible.*

    – Reb Alcé

'What is going on behind this door?'

'A book is shedding its leaves.'

'What is the story of the book?'

'Becoming aware of a scream.'

'I saw rabbis go in.'

'They are privileged readers. They come in small groups to give us
       their comments.'

'Have they read the book?'

'They are reading it.'

'Did they happen by for the fun of it?'

'They foresaw the book. They are prepared to encounter it.'

'Do they know the characters?'

'They know our martyrs.'

'Where is the book set?'

'In the book.'

'Who are you?'

'I am the keeper of the house.'

'Where do you come from?'

'I have wandered.'

'Is Yukel your friend?'

'I am like Yukel.'

'What is your lot?'

'To open the book.'

'Are you in the book?'

'My place is at the threshold.'

'What have you tried to learn?'

'I sometimes stop on the road to the sources and question the
    signs, the world of my ancestors.'
'You examine recaptured words.'
'The nights and mornings of the syllables which are mine, yes.'
'Your mind is wandering.'
'I have been wandering for two thousand years.'
'I have trouble following you.'
'I, too, have often tried to give up.'
'Do we have a tale here?'
'My story has been told so many times.'
'What is your story?'
'Ours, insofar as it is absent.'
'I do not understand.'
'Speaking tortures me.'
'Where are you?'
'In what I say.'
'What is your truth?'
'What lacerates me.'
'And your salvation?'
'Forgetting what I said.'
'May I come in? It is getting dark.'
'In each word there burns a wick.'
'May I come in? It is getting dark around my soul.'
'It is dark around me, too.'
'What can you do for me?'
'Your share of luck is in yourself.'
'Writing for the sake of writing does nothing but show contempt.'
'Man is a written bond and place.'
'I hate what is said in place I have left behind.'
'You trade in the future, which is immediately translated. What
    you have left is you without you.'
'You oppose me to myself. How could I ever win this fight?'
'Defeat is the price agreed on.'

'You are a Jew, and you talk like one.'

'The four letters J U I F which designate my origin are your four
fingers. You can use your thumb to crush me.'

'You are a Jew, and you talk like one. But I am cold. It is dark. Let
me come into the house.'

'There is a lamp on my table. And the house is in the book.'

'So I will live in the house after all.'

'You will follow the book, whose every page is an abyss where the
wing shines with the name.'

Aimé Césaire
1913–2008
From *Notebook of a Return to the Native Land*
Martinique
Translated by Clayton Eshleman

Aimé Césaire was, with Léopold Sédar Senghor and Léon-Gontron Damas, one of the original founders of the Négritude movement. Working across poetry, theatre, theory, and politics, Césaire's texts have become foundational to much of contemporary postcolonial theory. In this poem, we see the Césaire exploring the struggle between wanting to live in this world and anticipating the next.

At the end of daybreak burgeoning with frail coves, the hungry Antilles, the Antilles pitted with smallpox, the Antilles dynamited by alcohol, stranded in the mud of this bay, in the dust of this town sinisterly stranded.

At the end of daybreak, the extreme, deceptive desolate eschar on the wound of the waters; the martyrs who do not bear witness; the flowers of blood that fade and scatter in the empty wind like the screeches of babbling parrots; an aged life mendaciously smiling, its lips opened by vacated agonies; an aged poverty rotting under the sun, silently; an aged silence bursting with tepid pustules, the awful futility of our raison d'être.

At the end of daybreak, on this very fragile earth thickness exceeded in a humiliating way by its grandiose future – the volcanoes will explode, the naked water will bear away the ripe sun stains and nothing will be left but a tepid bubbling pecked at by sea birds – the beach of dreams and the insane awakening.

At the end of daybreak, this town sprawled-flat, toppled from its common sense, inert, winded under its geometric weight of an eternally renewed cross, indocile to its fate, mute, vexed no matter what, incapable of growing with the juice of this earth, self-conscious, clipped, reduced, in breach of fauna and flora.

Octavio Paz
1914–1998
'Brotherhood: Homage to Claudius Ptolemy'
Mexico
Translated by Eloisa Amezcua

*'Without understanding I get it' – perhaps a distillation of all of
the poets in this volume. To sit in bewilderment, astonishment,
wonder. To relish it, find meaning in that unknowing.*

Homage to Claudius Ptolemy

I'm man: I exist briefly
and the night is enormous.
But I look up:
the stars write.
Without understanding I get it:
I'm writing too
and in this very instant
someone is spelling me out.

Oodgeroo Noonuccal
1920–1993
'God's One Mistake'
Australia

Spiritual poetry is generally expected to praise the divine – so much so, in fact, that 'poetry of praise' is often used as a synonym. However, this poem doesn't seek to praise God, necessarily, but questions God's decision to make humans, to imbue them with free will..

God's One Mistake

It repenteth me that I have made man. – Genesis, 6

I who am ignorant and know so little,
So little of life and less of God,
This I do know
That happiness is intended and could be,
That all wild simple things have life fulfilled
Save man,
That all on earth have natural happiness
Save man.
Without books or schools, lore or philosophy
In my own heart I know
That hate is wrong,
Injustice evil.
Pain there must be and tears,
Sorrow and death, but not
Intolerance, unkindness, cruelty,
Unless men choose
The mean and base, which Nature never made,
But we alone.
And sometimes I will think that God looks down
With loving smile, saying,
'Poor child, poor child, maybe I was wrong
In planning for you reason and free will
To fashion your own life in your own way.
For all the rest
I settled and appointed as for children
Their simple days, but you
I gave the Godlike gift to choose,
Who were not wise – for see how you have chosen,
Poor child, alone among them all now
Unhappy on the earth.'

Paul Celan
1920–1970
'There was Earth in Them'
Romania
Translated by Aria Aber

*Paul Celan was a Jewish Romanian poet who suffered
unimaginable violence inside the Nazi death camps, including
the murder of his parents. Though he spoke a number of
languages fluently, he wrote his poems in German, the language
of his oppressors, of his parents' murderers; Anne Carson wrote
that he 'translated German using German.' This poem, like much
of Celan's work, seems to be trying to collapse language into what
lies beyond language, to collapse one world into the next.*

There was Earth in Them

There was earth in them and
They dug.

They dug and dug and they filled
the day and the night. And they didn't thank God,
who, according to rumor, wanted it all,
who, according to rumor, knew of it all.

They dug until they couldn't hear a thing;
they never reached wisdom, they didn't sing a song,
they didn't even invent any words.

They dug.

There came a silence, and there came a storm,
and there came all the seas.

I dig, you dig, and the worm digs, too,
and the singing there sings: they dig.

O someone, o none, o no one, o you:
Where did you go, when there's nowhere to go?

O you dig, and I dig, and I dig my way to you,
and the ring on our finger is glowing.

Paul Laraque
1920–2007
'Rainbow'
Haiti

*The final line of this poem calls to mind the ending of Rilke's
'Archaic Torso of Apollo': 'here there is no place / that does not see
you. You must change your life.'*

Rainbow

It's a ribbon tied to the rain's hair
It's a multicoloured belt round the waist of a little darling
It's a talisman to chase the evil eye away
It's a lasso round the sun's neck
to make him come back and light up the earth

Rainbow plunges behind mountains
they say it goes to drink
all the way down the head of the water
Ogun grumbles like bamboo
the siren went off to make love

Two little fish climb up
to watch Queen Simbi dance the *banda*
my hat fell into the sea
when a little breeze blows
all the boats' sails will swell

Rainbow is a bridle in the thunder's mouth
It's the fright pushing back wars
It's a shot of white rum after the cockfights
we can all beat the drums
sing the loas and dance voodoo
It's a sickle to weed out misery
It's a big collective to tear out poverty
to make water run in every garden
so hoes under the sun can throw off lightning
a collective reaching all the way to Guinea
all the way to the other side of the sea

a collective of comrades of every colour
to transform the earth
to tame the mean ones
to change our life

Nazik Al-Malaika
1923–2007
'Love Song for Words'
Iraq
Translated by Rebecca Carol Johnson

*The Iraqi modernist Nazik Al-Malaika, known for introducing
free verse to Arabic poetry, ends this piece with a couplet that
might well serve as a succinct crystallization of this entire
anthology.*

Love Song for Words

Why do we fear words
when they have been rose-palmed hands,
fragrant, passing gently over our cheeks,
and glasses of heartening wine
sipped, one summer, by thirsty lips?

Why do we fear words
when among them are words like unseen bells,
whose echo announces in our troubled lives
the coming of a period of enchanted dawn,
drenched in love, and life?
So why do we fear words?

We took pleasure in silence.
We became still, fearing the secret might part our lips.
We thought that in words laid an unseen ghoul,
crouching, hidden by the letters from the ear of time.
We shackled the thirsty letters,
we forbade them to spread the night for us
as a cushion, dripping with music, dreams,
and warm cups.

Why do we fear words?
Among them are words of smooth sweetness
whose letters have drawn the warmth of hope from two lips,
and others that, rejoicing in pleasure
have waded through momentary joy with two drunk eyes.
Words, poetry, tenderly
turned to caress our cheeks, sounds
that, asleep in their echo, lies a rich colour, a rustling,
a secret ardour, a hidden longing.

Why do we fear words?
If their thorns have once wounded us,
then they have also wrapped their arms around our necks
and shed their sweet scent upon our desires.
If their letters have pierced us
and their face turned callously from us
Then they have also left us with an oud in our hands
And tomorrow they will shower us with life.
So pour us two full glasses of words!

Tomorrow we will build ourselves a dream-nest of words,
high, with ivy trailing from its letters.
We will nourish its buds with poetry
and water its flowers with words.
We will build a balcony for the timid rose
with pillars made of words,
and a cool hall flooded with deep shade,
guarded by words.

Our life we have dedicated as a prayer
To whom will we pray . . . but to words?

Wisława Szymborska
1923–2012
'Astonishment'
Poland
Translated by Clare Cavanagh and Stanisław Baranczak

The inescapable, miraculous strangeness of our being here at all! That there are things called days in which we move our strange and clumsy bodies! That the earth is filled with animals covered with fur, scales! That there are trees sucking light from a star 93 million miles away and turning that light into sugar! How impossibly strange, all of it! This post-war Polish titan survived both Hitler and Stalin and still found her way to this indelible wonder.

Astonishment

Why after all this one and not the rest?
Why this specific self, not in a nest,
but a house? Sewn up not in scales, but skin?
Not topped off by a leaf, but by a face?
Why on earth now, on Tuesday of all days,
and why on earth, pinned down by this star's pin?
In spite of years of my not being here?
In spite of seas of all these dates and fates,
these cells, celestials and coelenterates?
What is it really that made me appear
neither an inch nor half a globe too far,
neither a minute nor aeons too early?
What made me fill myself with me so squarely?
Why am I staring now into the dark
and muttering this unending monologue
just like the growling thing we call a dog?

Zbigniew Herbert
'The Envoy of Mr Cogito'
1924–1998
Poland
Translated by Alissa Valles

*Some gallop through this world armed with weapons, broad
shields and sharpened lances, braced for endless and inescapable
violence. Others, like Zbigniew Herbert's character Mr Cogito,
walk through it armed only with 'old incantations of humanity
fables and legends'. This anthology is for the latter group.*

The Envoy of Mr Cogito

Go where the others went before to the dark boundary
for the golden fleece of nothingness your last reward

go upright among those who are down on their knees
those with their backs turned those toppled in the dust

you have survived not so that you might live
you have little time you must give testimony

be courageous when reason fails you be courageous
in the final reckoning it is the only thing that counts

and your helpless Anger – may it be like the sea
whenever you hear the voice of the insulted and beaten

may you never be abandoned by your sister Scorn
for informers executioners cowards – they will win
go to your funeral with relief throw a lump of earth
a woodworm will write you a smooth- shaven life

and do not forgive in truth it is not in your power
to forgive in the name of those betrayed at dawn

beware however of overweening pride
examine your fool's face in the mirror
repeat: I was called – was there no one better than I

beware of dryness of heart love the morning spring
the bird with an unknown name the winter oak
the light on a wall the splendor of the sky
they do not need your warm breath
they are there to say: no one will console you

Keep watch – when a light on a hill gives a sign – rise and go
as long as the blood is still turning the dark star in your breast
repeat humanity's old incantations fairy tales and legends
for that is how you will attain the good you will not attain
repeat great words repeat them stubbornly
like those who crossed a desert and perished in the sand

for this they will reward you with what they have at hand
with the whip of laughter with murder on a garbage heap

go for only thus will you be admitted to the company of cold skulls
to the company of your forefathers: Gilgamesh Hector Roland
the defenders of the kingdom without bounds and the city of ashes

Be faithful Go

Yehuda Amichai
1924–2000
'A Man in His Life'
Israel
Translated by Chana Bloch and Stephen Mitchell

One of the great Hebrew poets of the twentieth century, Amichai
writes that man's soul is 'very professional. / Only his body
remains forever / an amateur.' I can't personally testify to having
a professional soul, but as someone who constantly forgets his
own body, missing stairs and walking into low branches, I can
certainly testify to the amateur body bit.

A Man in His Life

A man doesn't have time in his life
to have time for everything.
He doesn't have seasons enough to have
a season for every purpose. Ecclesiastes
Was wrong about that.

A man needs to love and to hate at the same moment,
to laugh and cry with the same eyes,
with the same hands to throw stones and to gather them,
to make love in war and war in love.
And to hate and forgive and remember and forget,
to arrange and confuse, to eat and to digest
what history
takes years and years to do.

A man doesn't have time.
When he loses he seeks, when he finds
he forgets, when he forgets he loves, when he loves
he begins to forget.

And his soul is seasoned, his soul
is very professional.
Only his body remains forever
an amateur. It tries and it misses,
gets muddled, doesn't learn a thing,
drunk and blind in its pleasures
and its pains.

He will die as figs die in autumn,
Shrivelled and full of himself and sweet,
the leaves growing dry on the ground,
the bare branches pointing to the place
where there's time for everything.

Ingeborg Bachmann
1926–1973
'Every Day'
Austria
Translated by Michael Hamburger

*I think about this poem almost every day. How does one praise
the divine in a world where 'War is no longer declared, / only
continued'? What does the word 'divine' even mean in such a
world?*

Every Day

War is no longer declared,
only continued. The monstrous
has become everyday. The hero
stays away from battle. The weak
have gone to the front.
The uniform of the day is patience,
its medal the pitiful star of hope above the heart.

The medal is awarded
when nothing more happens,
when the artillery falls silent,
when the enemy has grown invisible
and the shadow of eternal armament
covers the sky.

It is awarded
for desertion of the flag,
for bravery in the face of friends,
for the betrayal of unworthy secrets
and the disregard
of every command.

Kim Nam-Jo
1927–
'Foreign Flags'
South Korea
Translated by Brother Anthony of Taize

*The powerful emptiness of flags. Perhaps that is what, to answer
Ingeborg Bachmann, one prays to in a world where 'War is no
longer declared, / only continued.' Kim Nam-Jo, a Catholic poet of
South Korea, shows us how spiritual and political desolation can
sometimes braid into a single all-encompassing loneliness.*

Foreign Flags

There I first glimpsed
such desolate loneliness.

Above the soaring towers of the old castle
at Heidelberg
a flag is waving
like a boat being rowed
like a windmill turning in the wind
waving on and on
until the threads grow thin
then casting away that body like a corpse
they raise a new flag

I wonder
what it's like to be up there all alone
in the sky with the drifting clouds,
what it's like
to be shaking all over, looking down
on the mutability of people and things?

There I first glimpsed
such adult prayer.

Kamau Brathwaite
1930–2020
'Bread'
Barbados

Since the earliest visionary poets, dreams have been a powerful bridge between this world and the others. In Brathwaite's poem we find the line between the dream world and the human world blurring away almost completely.

Bread

Slowly the white dream wrestle(s) to life

hands shaping the salt and the foreign cornfields
the cold flesh kneaded by fingers
is ready for the charcoal for the black wife

of heat the years of green sleeping in the volcano.
the dream becomes tougher. settling into its shape
like a bullfrog. suns rise and electrons
touch it. walls melt into brown. moving to crisp and crackle

breathing edge of the knife of the oven.
noise of the shop. noise of the farmer. market.
on this slab of lord. on this table w/ its oil-skin cloth
on this altar of the bone. this sacrifice of isaac. warm dead. warm
          merchandise. more than worn merchandise
life
itself. the dream of the soil itself
flesh of the god you break. peace to your lips. strife

of the multitudes who howl all day for its saviour
who need its crumbs as fish. flickering through their green element
need a wide glassy wisdom
to keep their groans alive

and this loaf here. life
now halted. more and more water add-
itive. the dream less clear. the soil more distant
its prayer of table. bless of lips. more hard to reach w/ penn-

ies. the knife
that should have cut it. the hands that should have broken open
        its victory
of crusts at your throat. balaam watching w/ red leak
-ing eyes. the rats

finding only this young empty husk
sharp-
ening their ratchets. your wife
going out on the streets. searching searching

her feet tapping. the lights of the motor-
cars watching watching round-
ing the shape of her girdle. her back naked

rolled into night into night w/out morning
rolled into dead into dead w/out vision
rolled into life into life w/out dream

Adonis
1930–
'The New Noah'
Syria
Translated by Shawkat M. Toorawa

The legendary Syrian poet Adonis is known for pushing buttons, subverting familiar tropes and legends. What would world religion look like today if Adonis's defiant Noah was the one we met in the Abrahamic scriptures?

The New Noah

1

We travel upon the Ark, in mud and rain,
Our oars promises from God.
We live – and the rest of Humanity dies.
We travel upon the waves, fastening
Our lives to the ropes of corpses filling the skies.
But between Heaven and us is an opening,
A porthole for a supplication.

'Why, Lord, have you saved us alone
From among all the people and creatures?
And where are you casting us now?
To your other Land, to our First Home?
Into the leaves of Death, into the wind of Life?
In us, in our arteries, flows a fear of the Sun.
We despair of the Light,
We despair, Lord, of a tomorrow
In which to start Life anew.

If only we were not that seedling of Creation,
Of Earth and its generations,
If only we had remained simple Clay or Ember,
Or something in between,
Then we would not have to see
This World, its Lord, and its Hell, twice over.'

2

If time started anew,
and waters submerged the face of life,
and the earth convulsed, and that god
rushed to me, beseeching, 'Noah, save the living!'
I would not concern myself with his request.
I would travel upon my ark, removing
clay and pebbles from the eyes of the dead.
I would open the depths of their being to the flood,
and whisper in their veins
that we have returned from the wilderness,
that we have emerged from the cave,
that we have changed the sky of years,
that we sail without giving in to our fears –
that we do not heed the word of that god.
Our appointment is with death.
Our shores are a familiar and pleasing despair,
a gelid sea of iron water that we ford
to its very ends, undeterred,
heedless of that god and his word,
longing for a different, a new, lord.

Christopher Okigbo
1932–1967
'Come Thunder'
Nigeria

This powerful, Ecclesiastic poem comes from one of the titans of twentieth-century global modernism, Christopher Okigbo. Though he had major ideological differences with Senghor and Césaire over the concept of Négritude, the three often read and published each other's work. Okigbo died in arms defending Nsukka, the small university town where he first fell in love with poetry.

Come Thunder

Now that the triumphant march has entered the last street
    corners,
Remember, O dancers, the thunder among the clouds . . .

Now that the laughter, broken in two, hangs tremulous between
    the teeth,
Remember, O dancers, the lightning beyond the earth . . .

The smell of blood already floats in the lavender-mist of the
    afternoon.
The death sentence lies in ambush along the corridors of power;
And a great fearful thing already tugs at the cables of the open air,
A nebula immense and immeasurable, a night of deep waters –
An iron dream unnamed and unprintable, a path of stone.

The drowsy heads of the pods in barren farmlands witness it,
The homesteads abandoned in this century's brush fire witness it:
The myriad eyes of deserted corn cobs in burning barns witness it:
Magic birds with the miracle of lightning flash on their feathers . . .

The arrows of God tremble at the gates of light,
The drums of curfew pander to a dance of death;

And the secret thing in its heaving
Threatens with iron mask
The last lighted torch of the century . . .

Ingrid Jonker
1933–1965
'There Is Just One Forever'
South Africa
Translated by Simone Jonker

*Though she died tragically at age thirty-one, Jonker left behind
a truly staggering body of poetic work. Sometimes I feel like
tattooing the final line of this poem across my forehead,
to remind myself.*

There Is Just One Forever

Ochre night and your hands
a vineyard through summer and frost?
eyes of rain over the meadows, but
there is just one forever

moment of your glittering body,
words without language – treachery
of your gleaming hands, because
there is just one forever

Green growth of the eternal
warmed cultivated and matured
great glow of the ochre earth, oh
there is just one forever

Jean Valentine
1934–2020
'The River at Wolf'
America

'Blessed are they who remember / that what they now have they
once longed for.' What's one thing you have in your life today that
you once only dreamed of? What's another?

The River at Wolf

Coming east we left the animals
pelican beaver osprey muskrat and snake
their hair and skin and feathers
their eyes in the dark: red and green.
Your finger drawing my mouth.

Blessed are they who remember
that what they now have they once longed for.

A day a year ago last summer
God filled me with himself, like gold, inside,
deeper inside than marrow.

This close to God this close to you:
walking into the river at Wolf with
the animals. The snake's
green skin, lit from inside. Our second life.

Kofi Awoonor
1935–2013
'At the Gates'
Ghana

Awoonor was a powerful Ghanaian poet, novelist, historian,
educator and politician. Reading this poem with his senseless
death in a 2013 terrorist attack in mind always makes me
emotional.

At the Gates

I do not know which god sent me,
to fall in the river
and fall in the fire.
These have failed.
I move into the gates
demanding which war it is;
which war it is?
the dwellers in the gates
answer us; we will let that war come
they whom we followed to come
sons of our own mothers and fathers
bearing upon our heads nothing
save the thunder that does roar
who knows when evil matters will come.

Open the gates!
It is Akpabli Horsu who sent me
Open the gates, my mother's children
and let me enter
our thunder initiates have run amok
and we sleep in the desert land
not moving our feet
We will sleep in the desert
guns in our hands we cannot fire
knives in our hands we cannot throw
the death of a man is not far away.

I will drink it; it is my god who gave it to me
I will drink this calabash
for it is god's gift to me
bachelor, never go too far
for the drummer boys will cook and let you eat.

Don't cry for me
my daughter, death called her
it is an offering of my heart
the ram has not come to stay
three days and it has gone
elders and chiefs whom will I trust
a snake has bitten my daughter
whom will I trust?
walk on gently; give me an offering
that I will give it to God
and he will be happy.

Uproot the yams you planted
for everything comes from God
it is an evil god who sent me
that all I have done
I bear the magic of the singer that has come
I have no paddle, my wish,
to push my boat into the river.

Adélia Prado
1935–
'Dysrhythmia'
Brazil
Translated by Ellen Doré Watson

The Brazilian mystic Adélia Prado, like Enheduanna or Rūmī
before her, understands that the body is our only available
technology for understanding what does not live in the body. 'It's
the soul that's erotic,' she asserts, just lines before writing of God's
wrath, children laughing, destiny.

Dysrhythmia

Old people spit with absolutely no finesse
and bicycles bully traffic on the sidewalk.
The unknown poet waits for criticism
and reads his verses three times a day
like a monk with his book of hours.
The brush got old and no longer brushes.
Right now what's important
is to untangle the hair.
We give birth to life between our legs
and go on talking about it till the end,
few of us understanding:
it's the soul that's erotic.
If I want, I put on a Bach aria
so I can feel forgiving and calm.
What I understand of God is His wrath;
there's no other way to say it.
The ball thumping against the wall annoys me,
but the kids laugh, contented.
I've seen hundreds of afternoons like today.
No agony, just an anxious impatience:
something is going to happen.
Destiny doesn't exist.
It's God we need, and fast.

Lucille Clifton
1936–2010
'my dream about God'
America

Genesis says that God created humans in his own image, but often it feels like it's happening the other way round. Clifton has a way of using superficially simple language to totally upend all our expectations of the world and what lies beyond it.

my dream about God

He is wearing my grandfather's hat.
He is taller than my last uncle.
when He sits to listen
He leans forward tilting the chair

where His chin cups in my father's hand.
it is swollen and hard from creation.
His fingers drum on His knee
dads stern tattoo.

and who do i dream i am
accepting His attentions?

i am the good daughter who stays at home
singing and sewing.
when i whisper He strains to hear me and
He does whatever i say.

Vénus Khoury-Ghata
1937–
From *She Says*
Lebanon
Translated by Marilyn Hacker

The former US Poet Laureate W. S. Merwin once said, of the social role of poetry, 'One is trying to say everything that can be said for the things that one loves while there's still time.' Reading Vénus Khoury-Ghata, I feel a sense of that rush, that urgent call to preserve in the poem what cannot be preserved on the earth.

She Says

On the dark landing of her dreams
there is that ploughshare which furrows the floor of her house
        going from the sink to the bed
where women and cats whelp to the great relief of the canary who
        announces births

The same ploughshare flakes away beneath the fig-tree since the
        man's arms rusted

Scraping clean the dead man and his tools is beyond her forces
December is longer than the whole winter
and rain falling upon rain keeps her from bending over in her sleep

You there!
she calls out at mealtimes to the invisible silhouette
leaning over the furrow
because the dead do sometimes bend

Mahmoud Darwish
1941–2008
'I Didn't Apologize to the Well'
Palestine
Translated by Fady Joudah

*'I broke the myth and I broke', writes Darwish, one of our great
poets of exile. How many times in my life I've felt completely
unmoored by the shattering of one of my beloved load-bearing
myths! How many myths we as a species tell ourselves about all
our various 'lands of peace'!*

I Didn't Apologize to the Well

I didn't apologize to the well when I passed the well,
I borrowed from the ancient pine tree a cloud
and squeezed it like an orange, then waited for a gazelle
white and legendary. And I ordered my heart to be patient:
Be neutral as if you were not of me! Right here
the kind shepherds stood on air and evolved
their flutes, then persuaded the mountain quail towards
the snare. And right here I saddled a horse for flying towards
my planets, then flew. And right here the priestess
told me: Beware of the asphalt road and the cars
and walk upon your exhalation. Right here
I slackened my shadow and waited, I picked the tiniest
rock and stayed up late. I broke the myth and I broke.
And I circled the well until I flew from myself
to what isn't of it. A deep voice shouted at me:
This grave isn't your grave. So I apologized.
I read verses from the wise holy book, and said
to the unknown one in the well: Salaam upon you the day
you were killed in the land of peace, and the day you rise
from the darkness of the well alive!

M. NourbeSe Philip
1947–
From *Zong!*
Trinidad and Tobago/Canada

Philip's masterpiece Zong! *takes as its central subject an eighteenth-century legal decision orbiting the murder of over 130 enslaved Africans aboard a British slave ship. The poem conjures and curses through song and incantation, mutilating and sublimating the violent language of empire into a kind of musical fugue, one that illuminates the 'untold story'. The resulting text is a profound communion with the dead, one that – in Philip's own words –'cannot be told yet must be told, but only through its un-telling'.*

Zong! #15

defend the dead

          weight of circumstance

ground

      to usual &

         etc

         where the ratio of just

in less than

      is necessary

           to murder

the subject in property

the save in underwriter

         where etc tunes justice

         and the *ratio* of murder

         is

         the usual in occurred

Akilah Falope Ouma Weke Jubade

                    the just in ration

                    the suffer in loss

                                    defend the dead

                                    the weight

                                                            in

circumstance

            ached in necessary

                                        the ration in just

            age the act in the *ave* to justice

Micere Ndale Omowunmi Ramla Ajani

Inrasara
1957–
From *Allegory of the Land*
Vietnam
Translated by Alec Schachner

The old story says that on the last day, the poet will look out over their fields and see the black clouds of death, the locusts and horsemen approaching. They will see that everyone, everything they have ever known is gone and that soon they will be, too. The poet will take it all in for a moment – one deep breath, maybe two – then they will walk back inside and close their door. They will fix the light, sit down at their writing table, and continue working on their latest draft.

1

Not a few friends have scolded me for wasting time on Cham poetry
    is there even a trifling scarcity of readers? Will there be anyone to
    remember?
yet I want to squander my entire life on it
      though there may only be around a quarter dozen people
          though there may only be one person
or even if there's not a single living soul.

2

One line of proverb – one verse of folk song
half a child's lullaby – one page of ancient poetry
I search and gather
like a child seeking a tiny pebble
(pebbles that adults carelessly step past)
to build a castle for only myself to live in
a castle one day they'll use for shelter from the rain – it's certain!

SOURCES

Adonis, 'The New Noah,' translated by Shawkat M. Toorawa, from *Poetry* 190, no 1 (April 2007): 21–23. Reprinted with the permission of the translator and The Wylie Agency UK for the author.

Delmira Agustini, 'Inextinguishables,' translated by Eloisa Amezcua. Reprinted with the permission of the translator.

'Against a Growth' (Anglo-Saxon Charm) from Royal MS. 4A.XIV, British Museum, translated by Jos Charles. (previously unpublished). Reprinted with the permission of the translator.

Anna Akhmatova, poems from *Complete Poems of Anna Akhmatova*, translated by Judith Hemschemeyer, edited and introduced by Roberta Reeder. Copyright © 1989, 1992, 1997 by Judith Hemschemeyer. Reprinted with the permission of The Permissions Company, LLC on behalf of Zephyr Press and Canongate Books.

Yosano Akiko, 'To punish,' translated by Sandford Goldstein and Seishi Shinodo, from *Tangled Hair: Selected Tanka from Midaregami*. Copyright © 2002 by Cheng & Tsui Company, Inc. Used by permission of Cheng & Tsui Company, Inc.

Nazik Al-Malaika. 'Love song for words,' translated by Rebecca Carol Johnson from Words Without Borders (October 2003). Reprinted with the permission of the translator.

Dante Alighieri, Canto III from *Inferno*, by translated by Mary Jo Bang. English translation copyright © 2012 by Mary Jo Bang. Reprinted with the permission of Graywolf Press, Minneapolis, Minnesota, graywolfpress.org.

Yehuda Amichai, 'A Man In His Life', translated by Chana Bloch and Stephen Mitchell, from *The Selected Poetry of Yehuda Amichai*. Reprinted by permission of the University of California Press.

Attar of Nishapur, 'Parable of the Dead Dervishes in the Desert', translated by Sholeh Wolpé, from *The Conference of the Birds*. Copyright © 2017 by Sholeh Wolpé. Used by permission of W. W. Norton & Company, Inc.

Kofi Awoonor, 'At the Gates' from *The Promise of Hope: New and Selected Poems 1964–2013*. Copyright © 2014 by the Board of Regents of the University of Nebraska. Reprinted by permission of the University of Nebraska Press.

Ingeborg Bachmann, 'Every Day', translated by Michael Hamburger, from Michael Hamburger and Christopher Middleton, eds., *Modern German Poetry* (New York: Grove Press, 1962). Originally in *The Malahat Review* 37 (January 1976). Reprinted with the permission of The Michael Hamburger Trust.

Matsuo Bashō, 'Death Song', translated by Kaveh Akbar. Reprinted with the permission of the translator. 'In Kyoto', translated by Jane Hirshfield. Reprinted with the permission of the translator.

Kamau Brathwaite, 'Bread' from *Born to Slow Horses*. Copyright © 2005 by Kamau Brathwaite Reprinted by permission of Wesleyan University Press.

Yosa Buson, ['A solitude'], ['looking at flowers'], and ['the worthless monk'], translated by Allan Persinger from *Foxfire: Selected Poems of*

Yosa Buson, a Translation (thesis, 2013). Reprinted with the permission of the translator.

C. P. Cavafy, 'Body, Remember,' from *C. P. Cavafy: Collected Poems*, translated by Edmund Keeley and Philip Sherrard. Copyright © 1992 by Edmund Keeley and Philip Sherrard. Reprinted by permission of Princeton University Press

Paul Celan, 'There Was Earth in Them,' translated by Aria Aber. Reprinted with the permission of the translator.

Aimé Césaire, excerpt from *Notebook of a Return to the Native Land*, translated by Clayton Eshleman and Annette Smith. Copyright © 2001 by Aimé Césaire. Published by Wesleyan University Press. Reprinted with permission.

Chandaka, 'Two Cosmologies' from *Sanskrit Love Poetry*, translated by W. S. Merwin and J. Moussaieff Masson. Copyright © 1977 by W. S. Merwin and J. Moussaieff Masson. Used by permission of The Wylie Agency, LLC.

Lucille Clifton, 'my dream about God' from *The Collected Poems of Lucille Clifton.* Copyright © 1987 by Lucille Clifton. Reprinted with the permission of The Permissions Company, LLC on behalf of BOA Editions Ltd., boaeditions.org.

Mahmoud Darwish, 'I Didn't Apologize to the Well,' translated by Fady Joudah, from *The Butterfly's Burden*, translated by Fady Joudah. Copyright © 2007 by Mahmoud Darwish. Translation copyright © 2007 by Fady Joudah. Reprinted with the permission of The Permissions Company, LLC on behalf of Copper Canyon Press, coppercanyonpress.org.

Emily Dickinson, 576 ['I prayed, at first, a little Girl,']. Reprinted by permission of the publishers and the Trustees of Amherst

College from *The Poems of Emily Dickinson*, edited by Thomas H. Johnson, Cambridge, Mass.: The Belknap Press of Harvard University Press, Copyright 1951, © 1955 by the President and Fellows of Harvard College. Copyright © renewed 1979, 1983 by the President and Fellows of Harvard College. Copyright 1914, 1918, 1919, 1924, 1929, 1930, 1932, 1935, 1937, 1942, by Martha Dickinson Bianchi. Copyright © 1952, © 1957, 1958, 1963, 1965, by Mary L. Hampson.

Enheduanna, from 'Hymn to Inanna', translated by Jane Hirshfield, from *Women in Praise of the Sacred: 43 Centuries of Spiritual Poetry by Women*, edited by Jane Hirshfield (New York: HarperCollins, 1994). Reprinted with the permission of the translator.

Faiz Ahmed Faiz, 'Before You Came', translated by Naomi Lazard, from *The True Subject: Selected Poems of Faiz Ahmed Faiz*. Copyright © 1988 by Princeton University Press, Reprinted by permission of Princeton University Press.

Francis of Assisi, 'The Canticle of the Sun', translated by Bill Barrett. Reprinted with the permission of the translator.

Mirza Ghalib, 'For the raindrop, joy is in entering the river', translated by Jane Hirshfield, from *The Paris Review*, Issue 115 (Summer 1990). Reprinted with the permission of the author.

Johann Wolfgang von Goethe, 'Wanderer's Nightsong II', translated by Richard Stokes, from *The Book of Lieder: The Original Texts of over 1000 Songs*. Copyright © 2005 by Richard Stokes. Reprinted by permission of Faber and Faber, Ltd.

Hafez, Ghazal 17, translated by Charles Upton. Reprinted with the permission of the translator.

Hanshan, XI: 'The peach petals would like to stay', translated by A.S. Kline, from Words from *Cold Mountain: Twenty-Seven Poems by Han-shan* (Poetry in Translation, 2006). Copyright © 2006. Reprinted by permission.

Zbigniew Herbert, 'The Envoy of Mr. Cogito', translated by Alissa Valles from *The Collected Poems 1956-1998* Copyright © 2007 by the Estate of Zbigniew Herbert. Translation copyright © 2007 by Alissa Valles. Reprinted by permission of HarperCollins Publishers and The Wylie Agency UK.

Nazim Hikmet, 'Things I Didn't Know I Loved', translated by Randy Blasing and Mutlu Konuk, from *Poems of Nazim Hikmet*. Copyright © 1994, 2002 by Randy Blasing and Mutlu Konuk. Reprinted by permission of Persea Books, Inc (New York), perseabooks.com. All rights reserved.

Hildegard of Bingen, 'Song to the Creator', translated by Barbara Newman, from *St. Hildegard of Bingen: Symposia, A Critical Edition of the Symphonia armonie celestium revelationum*, edited and translated by Barbara Newman. Copyright © 1989 by Cornell University. Used by permission of the publisher, Cornell University Press.

Kakinomoto Hitomaro, 'In praise of Empress Jito', translated by Geoffrey Bownas and Anthony Thwaite, from *The Penguin Book of Japanese Verse*. Copyright © Geoffrey Bownas and Anthony Thwaite published by Penguin Books 1964, 1998, Penguin Classics 2009. Reprinted by permission of Penguin Books Limited

Homer, excerpt from *The Odyssey*, translated by Emily Wilson, Copyright © 2017 by Emily Wilson. Used by permission of W. W. Norton & Company, Inc.

Wumen Huikai, 'Case 27: Not Mind, Not Buddha,' translated by Kōun Yamada, from *The Gateless Gate: The Classic Book of Zen Koans*. Copyright © 2004 by Kazue Yamada. Reprinted with the permission of The Permissions Company, LLC on behalf of Wisdom Publications, wisdompubs.org.

Al-Husayn ibn Ahmad ibn Khalawayh, excerpts from 'Names of the Lion,' translated by David Larsen. Copyright © 2017 by David Larsen. Reprinted with the permission of The Permissions Company, LLC on behalf of Wave Books, wavepoetry.com.

Inrasara, 'Allegory of the Land,' translated by Alec Schachner, from *The Purification Festival in April* (Vietnam: The Culture and Literature Publishing House, 2015). Reprinted with the permission of the author and translator.

Muhammad Iqbal, ['These are the days of lightning,'] from *Taking Issue and Allah's Answer*, translated by Mustansir Dalvi. Reprinted with the permission of Penguin Random House Pvt Ltd., India.

Kobayashi Issa, ['All the time I pray to Buddha'], ['Even with insects--'], and ['The snow is melting'], from *The Essential Haiku: Versions of Basho, Buson, and Issa*, edited and with an introduction by Robert Hass. Copyright 1994 by Robert Hass. Reprinted by permission of HarperCollins Publishers.

Edmond Jabès, 'At the Threshold of the Book,' translated by Rosmarie Waldrop, from *From the Book to the Book: An Edmond Jabès Reader*. Copyright © 1991 by Wesleyan University. Reprinted by permission of Wesleyan University Press.

Ingrid Jonker, 'There is just one forever,' translated by Simone Jonker from *Waterfall of Moss and Sun*. Reprinted with the permission of Minimal Press.

Kabir, 'Brother, I've seen some . . .' translated by Arvind Krishna Mehrotra, from 'Songs of Kabir' published in English by New York Review Books Classics. Translated by Arvind Krishna Mehrotra. Copyright © 2011 by Arvind Krishna Mehrotra. All rights reserved.

Vénus Khoury-Ghata, 'On the dark landing of her dreams' from 'She Says' in *She Says*, translated by Marilyn Hacker. Copyright © 1999 by Vénus Khoury-Ghata. English translation copyright © 2003 by Marilyn Hacker. Reprinted with the permission of The Permissions Company, LLC on behalf of Graywolf Press, graywolfpress.org.

Paul Laraque, 'Lakansyel / Rainbow,' translated by Boadiba and Jack Hirschman, from *Open Gate: An Anthology of Haitian Creole Poetry* (Curbstone Press, 2001). Copyright © 2001 Paul Laraque. Translation copyright © 2001 by Jack Hirschman and Boadiba. All rights reserved.

Li Po, 'Drinking Alone Beneath The Moon' (Part 1), translated by David Hinton, from *The Selected Poems of Li Po*. Copyright © 1996 by David Hinton. Reprinted by permission of New Directions Publishing Corp. and Carcanet Press, Ltd.

Li Qingzhao, 'Late Spring,' translated by Jiaosheng Wang from *Sino-Platonic Papers* 13 (October 1989). Reprinted with the permission of Victor H. Mair.

Federico Garcia Lorca, 'Farewell,' translated by Kaveh Akbar. Reprinted with the permission of the translator.

Lucretius, excerpt from *The Nature of Things*, translated by A. E. Stallings, published by Penguin Classics. Translation copyright © 2007 by A. E. Stallings, published by Penguin Classics 2007. Reprinted by permission of Penguin Books Limited.

Mahadeviyakka, 'I do not call it his sign,' translated by Jane Hirshfield, from *Women in Praise of the Sacred: 43 Centuries of Spiritual Poetry by Women*, edited by Jane Hirshfield (New York: HarperCollins, 1994). Reprinted with the permission of the translator.

Osip Mandelstam, 'O Lord, help me to live through this night—,' translated by Clarence Brown and W. S. Merwin, from *Selected Poems of Osip Mandelstam*. Copyright © 1973 by Clarence Brown and W. S. Merwin. Reprinted with the permission of Scribner, a division of Simon & Schuster, Inc. and The Wylie Agency, LLC. All rights reserved.

Mayan people, from *The Popol Vuh*, translated by Michael Bazzett. Copyright © 2018 by Michael Bazzett. Reprinted with the permission of The Permissions Company, LLC on behalf of Milkweed Editions. milkweed.org.

Mechtild of Megdeburg, 'Of all that God has shown me,' translated by Jane Hirshfield, from *Women in Praise of the Sacred: 43 Centuries of Spiritual Poetry by Women*, edited by Jane Hirshfield (New York: HarperCollins, 1994). Reprinted with the permission of the translator.

Czeslaw Milosz, 'Dedication'from *Selected and Last Poems 1931–2004*. Copyright © 1988, 1991, 1995, 2001, 2004, 2006 by The Czeslaw Milosz Estate. published by Allen Lane The Penguin Press 2001, Penguin Classics 2005. Reprinted by permission of HarperCollins Publishers and Penguin Books Limited.

Mirabai, 'O friend, understand: the body,' translated by Jane Hirshfield, from *Women in Praise of the Sacred: 43 Centuries of Spiritual Poetry by Women*, edited by Jane Hirshfield (New York: HarperCollins, 1994). Reprinted with the permission of the translator.

Gabriela Mistral, 'The Return,' translated by Ursula K. Le Guin, from *Selected Poems of Gabriela Mistral.* Copyright © 2003 by The University of New Mexico Press. Reprinted by permission.

Nahuatl People, Florentine Codex, [The Midwife Addresses the Woman Who Has Died in Childbirth], translated by John Bierhorst. Copyright © 1994 by John Bierhorst. Reprinted with the permission of the translator.

Kim Nam-Jo, 'Foreign Flags,' translated by Brother Anthony of Taize. Reprinted with the permission of the translator.

Nezahualcoyotl, excerpts from 'The Painted Book,' translated by Miguel León-Portilla, from *Native Mesoamerican Spirituality.* Copyright © 1980 by The Missionary Society of St. Paul the Apostle in the State of New York. Reprinted with the permission of Paulist Press. paulistpress.com.

Oodgeroo Noonuccal, 'God's One Mistake' from *The Dawn Is At Hand.* Reprinted with the permission of Marion Boyars Publishers, London.

Christopher Okigbo, 'Come Thunder' from *Labyrinths & Path of Thunder.* Reprinted with the permission of the Christopher Okigbo Foundation.

Ono No Kamachi, ['This inn'], translated by Jane Hirshfield, from *The Ink Dark Moon: Love Poems by Onono Komachi and Izumi Shikibu.* Copyright © 1988 by Jane Hirshfield. Used by permission of Vintage Books, an imprint of the Knopf Doubleday Publishing Group, a division of Penguin Random House LLC. All rights reserved.

Patacara, 'When They Plow their Fields' translated by Susan Murcott, from *First Buddhist Women: Poems and Stories of Awakening.*

Copyright © 1991, 2006 by Susan Mucott. Reprinted with the permission of Parallax Press.

Octavio Paz, 'Brotherhood: Homage to Claudius Ptolemy,' translated by Eloisa Amezcua. Reprinted with the permission of the translator.

Walatta Petros, 'Our Mother Drives Demons Away from a Royal Woman' from *The Life and Struggles of Our Mother Walatta Petros: A Seventeenth-Century African Biography of an Ethiopian Woman*, translated by Wendy Laura Belcher and Michael Kleiner. Copyright © 2015 by Princeton University Press. Reprinted by permission of Princeton University Press.

M. NourbeSe Philip, 'Zong! #15' and 'Zong! #18' from *Zong!*, as told to the author by Setaey Adamu Boateng. Copyright © 2008 by M. NourbeSe Philip. Published by Wesleyan University Press and reprinted by permission.

Adelia Prado, 'Dysrhythmia,' translated by Ellen Doré Watson, from *The Mystical Rose: Selected Poems*. Reproduced with permission from Bloodaxe Books, Ltd., bloodaxebooks.com.

Rabi'a al-Basri, [Oh my Lord], translated by Charles Upton. Reprinted with the permission of the translator.

Rainer Maria Rilke, 'Second Elegy' from *Duino Elegies*, translated by David Young. Copyright © 1978 by W. W. Norton & Company, Inc. Used by permission of W. W. Norton & Company, Inc.

Rumi, 'Lift Now the Lid of the Jar of Heaven,' from *Teachings of Rumi*, re-created and edited by Andrew Harvey. Copyright ©1999 by Andrew Harvey. Reprinted by arrangement with The Permissions Company,

LLC on behalf of Shambhala Publications Inc., Boulder, Colorado, shambhala.com.

Saadi Shirazi, 'The Grass Cried Out,' translated by Kaveh Akbar. Reprinted with the permission of the translator.

María Sabina, from 'The Midnight Velada,' translated by Eloisa de Estrada Gonzales and Henry Munn in *New Wilderness Letter* nos. 5–6 (1978). Reprinted by permission.

St. John of the Cross, 'Love's Living Flame,' translated by Antonio de Nicolás, from *St. John of the Cross (San Juan De La Cruz): Alchemist of the Soul: His Life, His Poetry, His Prose*. Copyright © 1989 by Antonio T de Nicolás. Reprinted with the permission of Red Wheel/Weiser.

Sappho, Fragments 22 and 118 translated by Anne Carson from *If Not, Winter: Fragments of Sappho*. Copyright © 2002 by Anne Carson. Used by permission of Alfred A. Knopf, an imprint of the Knopf Doubleday Publishing Group, a division of Penguin Random House LLC and Little Brown and Company UK. All rights reserved.

Sengcan, 'The Mind of Absolute Trust,' translated by Stephen Mitchell, from *The Enlightened Heart: An Anthology of Sacred Poetry*. Copyright © 1989 by Stephen Mitchell. Reprinted by permission of HarperCollins Publishers.

Leopold Sédar Senghor, 'Totem' from *The Collected Poetry of Leopold Sédar Senghor*, edited and translated by Melvin Dixon. Copyright © 1991 by Melvin Dixon. Reprinted by permission of the University of Virginia Press.

Shenoute, 'Homily,' translated by Kaveh Akbar. Reprinted with the permission of the translator.

Edith Södergran, 'A Life,' translated by Averill Curdy, from Poetry (March 2012). Reprinted with the permission of the translator.

Sor Juana Inés de la Cruz, 'Suspend, singer Swan, the sweet accent,' translated by Eloisa Amerzcua. Reprinted with the permission of the translator.

'The Epic of Sundiata' from *Sundiata: A West African Epic of the Mande Peoples*, translated by David C. Conrad and narrated by Djanka Tassey Condé. Copyright © 2004 by Hackett Publishing Company, Inc. Reprinted with the permission of Hackett Publishing Company, Inc.

Izumi Shikibu, 'Things I Want Decided,' translated by Jane Hirshfield, from *The Ink Dark Moon: Love Poems by Onono Komachi and Izumi Shikibu*. Copyright © 1988 by Jane Hirshfield. Used by permission of Vintage Books, an imprint of the Knopf Doubleday Publishing Group, a division of Penguin Random House LLC. All rights reserved.

Wislawa Szymborska, 'Astonishment,' translated by Clare Cavanagh and Stanislaw Baranczak, from *Poems New and Collected 1957–1997*. English translation copyright © 2015 by Houghton Mifflin Harcourt Publishing Company. Reprinted by permission of Houghton Mifflin Harcourt Publishing Company. All rights reserved.

Teresa of Avila, 'Laughter Came from Every Brick,' from *Love Poems from God: Twelve Sacred Voices from East and West*, translated by Daniel Ladinsky (New York: Penguin, 2002). Reprinted with the permission of the translator.

Marina Tsvetaeva, from 'Poems to Czechia' from *Dark Elderberry Branch: Poems of Marina Tsvetaeva: A Reading by Ilya Kaminsky and Jean Valentine*. Copyright © 2012 by Ilya Kaminsky and Jean Valentine. Reprinted with the permission of The Permissions Company, LLC on behalf of Alice James Books, alicejamesbooks.org.

Lao Tzu, 'Easy by nature' from *Tao Te Ching: A New English Version*, by Ursula K. Le Guin, © 1997 by Ursula K. Le Guin. Reprinted by arrangement with The Permissions Company, LLC on behalf of Shambhala Publications, Inc., shambhala.com.

Unknown, '(Death of Enkidu)' from *The Epic of Gilgamesh, Second Revised Edition*, translated by N. K. Sandars, published by Penguin Classics. Translation copyright © 1959, 1960, 1964, 1972 by N. K. Sandars, published by Penguin Books 1960, Penguin Classics 1973, 1985, 2003. Reprinted by permission of Penguin Books Limited.

Unknown, 'Egyptian God Names' from *The Book of the Dead*, translated by Alexandre Piankoff, from *The Shrines of Tut-Ankh-Amon*. Copyright © 1955 by Bollingen Foundation, Inc., New York. Reprinted by permission of Princeton University Press.

Uvavnuk, 'The great Sea,' translated by Jane Hirshfield, from *Women in Praise of the Sacred: 43 Centuries of Spiritual Poetry by Women*, edited by Jane Hirshfield (New York: HarperCollins, 1994). Reprinted with the permission of the translator.

Jean Valentine, 'The River at Wolf' from *The River at Wolf*. Copyright © 1992 by Jean Valentine. Reprinted with the permission of The Permissions Company, LLC on behalf of Alice James Books, alicejamesbooks.org.

Virgil, Book 1: Neptune Intervenes from *The Aeneid: A New Translation*, translated Sarah Ruden. Copyright © 2008 by Yale University Press. Reprinted by permission of Yale University Press.

Vyasa, excerpts from 'The Third Discourse' from *The Bhagavad Gita*, translated by Laurie Patton, published by Penguin Classics. Translation copyright © Laurie L. Patton 2008, published by Penguin Classics 2008. Reprinted by permission of Penguin Books Limited.

355

Xu Zhimo, 'Second Farewell to Cambridge' translated by Michelle Yeh, from *Anthology of Modern Chinese Poetry*. Copyright © 1992 by Yale University. Reprinted by permission of Yale University Press.

Yaqui People, 'Deer Song' from *Yaqui Deer Songs, Maso Bwikam*, edited by Larry Evers and Felipe S. Molina. Copyright © 1987 The Arizona Board of Regents. Reprinted with the permission of The University of Arizona Press.

Yoruba People, excerpt from *A Recitation of Ifa, Oracle of the Yoruba*, translated by Awotunde Aworinde, John Olaniyi Ogundipe and Judith Gleason (Grossman, 1973).

ACKNOWLEDGEMENTS

This anthology stems directly from a graduate seminar I taught at Purdue University in Spring 2018 called 'Writing the Divine.' Every student in that course illuminated, complicated, and deepened this text – I thank them each and all. I'd like to especially thank Noah Baldino, Javan DeHavan, Jennifer Loyd, and Caleb Milne for their immeasurable help in the early stages of permissions acquisitions. Thanks to Frederick Courtright for finishing that dizzying endeavour for us. Thank you to the entire Penguin family for believing in this project and helping to run it up the mountain. Thank you to all the poets and translators included here for the profound gift of their work. Special thanks to Jane Hirshfield, whose curatorial work and translations have been so instrumental in the conception and execution of this anthology. Finally, massive thanks to my editor Maria Bedford, whose singular vision and herculean patience allowed this project to find its potential.

INDEX OF FIRST LINES

Just these two words He spoke 135

Lady of all powers, 3
Looking at flowers 174
Lord, who createdst man in wealth and store, 157

Most high, all powerful, all good Lord! All praise is
    yours, 85

Naked we return to our Master, 235
Not a few friends have scolded me for wasting time on
    Cham poetry 337
Now that the triumphant march has entered the last street
    corners 315
Now we will further tell you about our holy mother Walatta
    Petros 159

O friend, understand: the body 127
O Lord, help me to live through this night 245
O Love's living flame, 139
O my Lord, 63
O thou bright jewel in my aim I strive 185
O, for that warning voice, which he, who saw 161
Ochre night and your hands 317
Of all that God has shown me 93
Oh, you who sleep so deep you do not wake! 299
Old people spit with absolutely no finesse 325
On the dark landing of her dreams 329
Our great Empress 59
Over every mountain-top 183

Poor soul, the centre of my sinful earth, 149
Pour, cupbearer, the wine of the invisible, 91
Precious feather, child, 153

Regarding the sinners, 51

'Sire,' announced the servant to the King, 'the saint Narottam
    never 215
Slowly the white dream wrestle(s) to life 307
Softly I am leaving, 255
Suspend, singer swan, the sweet strain: 171

That the stars are adamant 247
The clepsydra has stopped dripping; 77
The day was over. Jove looked down from heaven 47
The Frenchmen asked my father (Naamu) 113
The goddess Laksmi 33
The great sea 211
The Great Way isn't difficult 53
The Lord is my shepherd; I shall not want. 19
The morning blossoms, and immediately the cloud
    conceals it 115
The one who does not 37
The peach petals would like to stay, 67
The snow is melting 193
The song of songs, which is Solomon's. 15
The world is charged with the grandeur of God. 213
The worthless monk 175
There he comes out, 119
There I first glimpsed 305
There was earth in them and 283
These are the days of lightning, 225
This day on which Enkidu dreamed came to an end and he lay 7
This inn 65
'This is absurd, 21
Thou still unravish'd bride of quietness, 197
To punish 227
To see a World in a Grain of Sand 187

INDEX OF TITLES

On Virtue 185